WHY GOD SPOKE TO ME

Dr. Zuckerman's God Scripted Path to Redemption & Enlightenment

Stephen Zuckerman, M.D.

Copyright © 2016 by Stephen L. Zuckerman, M.D.

A Top Pick Publication

All rights reserved.

TOP PICK INC
964 Ringenbach Street
Chaska, Minnesota 55318

Co-Editors-Rachel Carter & Stephanie Ericcson

Front book Cover Original Art: "Genesis" 9-23-2013 Aribert Munzner
Back Book Cover Photo Credit: Joshua R. Zuckerman

All rights reserved, which includes the right to reproduce this book or portions thereof in any form whatsoever except as provided by the U.S. Copyright Law.

For information or reprint permission, contact:

TOP PICK INC
customersupport@toppickink.com
www.toppickink.com
or
www.zuckerisms.com

First printing January 2017

License Notes

This book is licensed for your personal enjoyment only. It may not be resold or given away. If you would like to share this book with another person, please purchase an additional copy for each recipient. Thank you for respecting the hard work of this author.

Names have been changed to protect the innocent.

To Gabriel Kirschenbaum, the most outrageous of physicians.

After a brief encounter at birth, I met him formally at age 2.5. From then on I wanted to be an outrageous physician too.

Table of Contents

Chapter 1: Trouble 1
Chapter 2: The First Day 7
Chapter 3: The Second Day 20
Chapter 4: The Third Day 28
Chapter 5: The Spoken Word 34
Chapter 6: The Slime Mold 38
Chapter 7: The Plot Thickens 50
Chapter 8: Psychiatry Enters, Stage Left 59
Chapter 9: Meeting Madelaine (Captivated) 64
Chapter 10: The Halcyon Years 70
Chapter 11: Joel Black Knife And The Mrs. 76
Chapter 12: On The Road With Mrs. Black Knife 84
Chapter 13: Madelaine Returns 91
Chapter 14: Africa 100
Chapter 15: Attack Of The Dybbuk 112
Chapter 16: Six Psychic Sessions To Love 118
Chapter 17: The Computer Schism 127
Chapter 18: Incarceration 133
Chapter 19: Life In The University Hospital Psych Ward
 146
Chapter 20: Revelation 153
Chapter 21: Revelation 2 158
Chapter 22: Asylum 170
Chapter 23: Early Fall, 1991 185

Chapter 24: Epiphany 208
Epilogue 228
The Horse Race 230
Acknowledgements 231
Biography 233

Introduction, by Stephanie Ericsson

When I began working with Dr. Stephen Zuckerman in 1998 on his first book, it quickly became apparent that his ideas were multilayered, often built upon one another—even, at times, holographic in their dimensions. These were concepts that pummeled at comfortable paradigms to make way for *new* ways of thinking. Some were not really so new but rather more complete, or more compassionate, or farther reaching.

It is the mark of an enduring idea when it continues to bear fruit even after many pluckings. After years of working with Dr. Zuckerman, I am *still* discovering layers of meaning within his words and concepts that on first, second, or even third glance had escaped me. Many of his ideas and concepts are disguised in such simplicity that it is easy to believe one caught the entire meaning right away. Yet again and again, surprising *ah ha's!* have burst upon me from writings that I thought I'd understood in total. The interconnection of one idea to another, or a larger meaning tucked into a goofy word-play, or a concept that suddenly offered a new tool for dealing with some private torment of my own—

these experiences have captivated me as much as a reader as they have as his editor.

The most challenging of Zuckerman's experiences was his claim of having conversed with the voice of G-d for a period of time just after he turned fifty. Who, in their right mind, would believe such a thing? Certainly no one who values their credibility! Not other doctors, not psychiatrists, not upstanding businessmen or any one in today's techno-culture. While this voice succeeded in getting him incarcerated in his own Kesey-ian *Cuckoo's Nest,* it also proved to be a brilliant co-conspirator, taskmaster, conscience, mentor, and spiritual guru. It succeeded in testing the medical legal system, the patience of his associates, and the odds at the racetrack. It outsmarted doctors, judges, and the DMS-4. It forced him to throw his professional and personal credibility to the dogs and literally got him a prognosis so hopeless that he spent three months in the kind of state institution where most inmates never leave. Even so, in taking so much from him, it did not leave him bankrupt.

When Zuckerman first described The Voice and the story of his encounter with G-d, I had a difficult time believing that he was fully sane. But over time, I found that there was nothing about him that supported those doubts. Nothing in his past history, his medical or familial history supported the diagnosis of psychosis. He'd lived a life that was relatively unscathed by misfortune—no physical or emotion abuse from childhood that pointed toward the pathological. Nor was he religiously fanatical, or religiously savvy, for that matter. He'd been raised by his parents as a secular Jew—typical of their generation—who attended synagogue once a year on Yom Kippur, held a Seder at Passover, and the rest of the time worked long, hard hours to provide opportunities for his children. He'd never been traumatized like so many men of his generation who'd been drafted into the insanity of Vietnam. And although he was passionate about his work, he wasn't driven to obsession, but rather led a balanced life most people would have envied for its sanity. He had no history of alcohol or drug abuse and he was physically fit and had been healthy his entire life.

His parents loved him and raised him in relative middle class comfort so he wasn't tormented by the privation of poverty as so many Jewish families had been during and after World War II. His sense of humor and playful nature seemed to make his long hours as a doctor not only bearable, but thoroughly enjoyable. He had endless patience, was quick to forgive, slow to judge, and nearly impossible to rouse to anger. Although he was brilliant, his wasn't a tormented intelligence, as so many highly gifted people suffer from. In short, there was nothing that pointed to Stephen Zuckerman as a nutcase.

His description of The Voice, both in conversations and in his writing, were always consistent, never indulgent or dramatic, and just quirky enough to be believable.

But, if I were to "believe" his story, I found that I had to do so on more than just a personal level—as his editor, I had to believe him on a professional level as well. Otherwise I would find myself either condescending to him as my client, or be entirely unable to work with him. I had to suspend the part of me that was agnostic. I had to challenge the skeptic modernist in me while calling on the Catholic training of my childhood. I read everything I could find that might lead me to the key. I wrote in my own personal journal about it, and even went back to the church. I meditated on Dr. Zuckerman's words and secretly hoped that Zuckerman's G-d would pay me a visit too. I spoke to mystics and found that visions and apparitions were more of a pain than a blessing and anyone with any sense would not wish for one. St. John of the Cross and St. Teresa of Avila had said the same thing about their experiences.

Ultimately, it was a matter of letting go of my blocks to believe and having the courage to simply listen to the message. Did it make sense? Did it sound real? Did it speak to me?

These are the questions that anyone who picks up this book will have to answer for themselves. Some of what Zuckerman describes is supported in scripture, tradition, and history and some will be debatable.

And so, Gentle Reader, in the end, it will be as it always has been—a matter of faith.

Chapter 1: Trouble

When I wrote down my to-do list that day in May of '91, it did not include

getting arrested and thrown into a locked psyche ward. *My* plan had been to retrieve the computer my ex-girlfriend, Madelaine, had talked me into buying in exchange for work she'd never delivered. I'd been patient. I'd been understanding. I'd been forgiving. But it became clear that she had played me. That day I decided to stop being her doormat.

I called Madelaine to tell her I was coming over and somehow our conversation ended with me shouting, "I'm gonna kill your ass!" An hour later there was a knock on my door. It was my brother, who had come all the way from Texas without warning, making some vague excuse for being there. I told him I was busy—I needed to go get my computer. He offered to drive, so off we went in his rental car. In the wrong direction.

"Where are you going? I told you she lives the other way," I said to him. He ignored me and just kept driving.

"Are you hard of hearing, Bobby? Turn around and go that way." He kept going in the wrong direction. Now I was annoyed.

"Look, if you're not going to take me there, let me out here and I'll walk back to my place and take my own car."

He made no move to turn the car around.

"I said, PULL OVER!" I shouted, but he stayed silent. I couldn't understand why he wouldn't listen to me.

The traffic in front of us slowed down for a red light. I saw my chance and jumped out of the car. It was only five blocks back to my place, but I was glad to be able to walk off my rage. What the hell was his story, anyway?!

I don't get angry much as a rule, and I knew I needed to calm down. I sat in my kitchen and thought, *it's probably not a good idea to go over to Madelaine's all riled up*. Not after the screamer we'd had earlier, anyway. So I decided to head for the racetrack instead.

There, I spent the afternoon schmoozing with a few cronies and losing a few bucks, which was just what I needed to put my head back together. After the races I headed home for a nap.

Loud knocking woke me up and I opened the front door to two uniformed police officers.

"Are you Stephen Zuckerman?" they asked. I said I was. They asked if they could come in for a moment, so I opened the door, wondering if one of my neighbors had been robbed or something. They were friendly, almost too casual—talking about the weather, asking me how I was doing.

I made some joke the way I always do, and one of them said,

"There are some folks who are worried about you, Dr. Zuckerman."

"What are they worried about?"

"Well, they're concerned about your health and wanted to make sure that you're okay."

"Really? What people are you talking about?" I asked.

"We were asked to take you over to Hennepin County Medical Center so they can check you out."

"Really? You guys make house calls? Don't you have some more important work to do? I'm really fine...."

The officers exchanged glances, and then one of them said, "Nah, you see, we promised. So, why don't you just come with us now and we'll get you checked out. It won't take long. You don't have any place you have to be for an hour or so, do you?"

Something in me stopped protesting. I haven't had much exposure to policemen, but it was clear that they were going to take me whether I was willing or not. Since I preferred not to find out what handcuffs felt like, I went with them.

I had no idea, at that time, that behind my back, a conspiracy was fermenting. My brother, Madelaine, my business partner, Sid—hell, even my mother back in Queens—had all been in on the plot they called an intervention. Not the kind you do with alcoholics and drug addicts, but the kind you do when someone cracks up.

Over the next few months, I got a quick and dirty introduction into the black hole of American psychiatry's version of extraordinary rendition. That word wouldn't become a household term for another ten years, until after 9/11 and Guantanamo Bay, but soon I would become intimately acquainted with its meaning.

It's not that I was tortured, at least not physically, but I would be imprisoned behind a locked door, without shoelaces to hang myself with, without sharp things to slit my wrists with and without a voice to raise in protest. All those trivial freedoms we take for granted everyday—what socks to wear, what route to bike to work, when and what to eat, who to call that day and who to dodge—were stripped away.

I didn't realize how glorious it is to simply be able to walk out of my own house and go where I want. Like air, we don't notice how very nice it is until we don't have any.

In lockup, there were cameras that recorded my every move, giant men without necks in blue scrubs who guarded the exits and who followed me into the men's room—I assume because they were afraid I'd try to drown myself in the urinal. The only reading materials were pamphlets with titles like, *Am I borderline?* Or *I'm OK, But You're a Jerk*, and a TV in the corner that was turned up to its loudest setting, always stationed on one sports channel or another.

Williams S. Burroughs once said, "A paranoid is someone who knows a little of what's going on." I would soon understand exactly what he meant.

Chapter 2: The First Day

My life began falling apart in the fall of 1990 when I was getting close to turning fifty. Seventeen years before, I'd left medicine to do medical missionary work in central Minnesota, after which I started my own venture capital business. Medicine was always my first love, so I kept my medical license current every year. I found investing in new medical start-ups incredibly exciting and I was good at it. But as fifty approached, my work running venture capital funds and start-up companies had stagnated. Worse, I had none of my former enthusiasm. I was drained. All of the motivation that had made work so enjoyable—raising capital, pursuing investors, searching out nascent medical technologies with all the right stuff—was gone.

When my girlfriend of five years, Madelaine, broke off our relationship with, "I don't want to sleep with you anymore," I plummeted into a depression that I couldn't seem to crawl out of. I don't mean that I was just blue or sad like I'd been at various points in my life. During those times I'd be out of sorts for a few days before returning to my old self. This time I was shrinking inward.

I was no longer sure there was an old self to return to. The whole world seemed out of kilter, like I had just stepped into *The Cabinet of Dr. Caligari*. Everything was skewed—redrawn by some architect with a twisted sense of humor.

Strange sensations began to overwhelm me. Some were bodily sensations, some sensual, and almost all of them had an otherworldly feel to them. I was still me, and yet, I wasn't. I was seeing things around me as if I was seeing them for the very first time—things that must have been there all along but I'd never noticed them before. My hearing tuned itself to a higher frequency. I suddenly noticed things like the whirl of the air in my good ear as I walked around the city lakes of Minneapolis. My vision telescoped in on details I had never bothered to notice—the throat of a bird, the luminescence of a flower, the music that clouds make. Sometimes, they were so poignant that tears would come to my eyes. Even my thoughts didn't seem wholly my own anymore.

Looking back now, I know that I had suddenly become aware of the invisible aspect of our world—those unseen, unheard, unprovable things that exist all around us. At times I could envision events happening elsewhere. While getting a haircut in downtown Minneapolis I had a vision of a female police officer writing a parking ticket on my car which was parked around the corner from the barber shop. I jumped out of the barber chair and raced around the corner to my car and sure enough there was the lady officer starting to write me a ticket.

Other times when I was in intimate conversation with a good friend, looking into their eyes, my vision would become blurred. I would feel us "coming together," as though our minds were suddenly merged.

Other incidents were almost comical, like the powerful pain I had if I snuck a late-night nosh from the fridge that shot up from the wart on my left big toe. If I began to lie or exaggerate about something, I would suddenly drop words out of my sentences, forcing myself to start the sentence all over. Worse, until I told the truth, it kept happening. Once, on a Sunday morning while I was cleaning my kitchen, I had a premonition that a horse I'd never heard of was going to win a Pick

Six race at Golden Gate Fields in California, a race I could bet on by simulcast at Canterbury Downs, the local track for Minneapolis-St. Paul. I actually went to the track thinking, *Can this be for real?* Sure enough, not only did the horse exist, but it was running at 7 to 1 odds. I laid down a bet of $50 to win and came away $350 richer. So, I wondered, is it possible to know the future? If, as Einstein's theory of relativity claimed, there was no such thing as linear time and everything is happening all at once—past, present, and future—did this explain what was happening to me?

Then, one night in April, 1991, while lying in bed floating in that delicious limbo between wakefulness and sleep, I heard a voice speak to me in my deaf ear.

I froze. I had not heard a single sound in that ear for twenty-five years. As a physician, I know that it is impossible to have a spontaneous return of hearing with otosclerosis, or frozen ear bones. These body parts do not regenerate themselves.

But, there it was—a voice—as distinct as if it were speaking into my good ear.

Without any obvious accent, it commanded me:

"GO TO YOUR BATHROOM AND FACE THE WALL, DAMMIT! AND DON'T TURN ON THE LIGHT, YOU LITTLE SCHMUCK."

Stunned, my thoughts raced to adjust to this totally unanticipated, altogether alien assault and I fumbled for a rational explanation.

Who...WHAT is this? Had an alien from outer space entered me? Was it G-d? Nah, it couldn't be...or maybe it could. After all, G-d spoke to human beings in the Old Testament all the time. But, wait a minute—those conversations didn't actually happen, did they? Am I going crazy? Hearing voices like some schizophrenic who thinks G-d, Morgan Freeman, or the devil is singling him out for a special message? But then, I thought, how could I be crazy if I was lucid enough to know that the sudden manifestation of a voice in my deaf ear could be a symptom of insanity?

No question about it—I was scared shitless. But I was thrilled too.

"GO TO YOUR BATHROOM!" The Voice demanded. "GET MOVING! NOW!"

I scrambled into the bathroom and fumbled in the dark, feeling for the wall.

"CLOSE YOUR EYES AND FACE THE WALL. DO IT NOW, DAMMIT!" it yelled. I put my nose against the wall and waited, my heart pounding. I thought how ridiculous I must look. Anyone watching would think I'd lost my mind.

I closed my eyes. What was it going to do to me? If this was G-d, could He really be cursing? I had not thought much about G-d in my life, but I never imagined Him swearing like a garment-center worker.

"I WILL REVEAL MYSELF TO YOU," The Voice thundered.

Oh shit, Stephen, this is bad, I thought. You actually think you're hearing a voice in your deaf ear. And not just any voice…. No, no, you think you're hearing G-d's voice.

Every doctor knows that hearing voices others don't is the most common form of hallucination associated with a psychotic-break—the one indisputable symptom that can confirm insanity. Absurd images raced through my head in a matter of a split second: a random scene from *One Flew Over the Cuckoo's Nest*, a memory of an old friend doing the Haldol shuffle, flashes of patients with facial tics and the

Rabbit Syndrome, their mouths and tongues wracked with tremors. But the alien voice didn't give me time to linger.

"GO BACK TO YOUR BED, LAY DOWN AND CLOSE YOUR EYES. I AM GOING TO TAKE YOU ON A TRIP THROUGH THE UNIVERSE."

Well, at least it's not telling me to bomb the Pentagon. I hurried back to my bed and assumed the position. *A trip through the universe, huh?* Sounds exciting.

Into what I can only describe as my "mind's eye" came a series of cosmic images. The first few were a real letdown; I'd expected something spectacular, galactic, celestial, but they were humdrum, two-dimensional still images. Moments from my life, pictures of nature, a tree bending in the wind.

I yawned. You'd think they'd have a little more pizzazz. But The Voice was probably just getting warmed up. They'd get better, I figured.

But they didn't. The images looked more like they'd been taken from my old second-grade science primer—published before satellites, before Hubble, before high-speed photography.

This is pathetic, I thought, G-d needs to get Himself a new media consultant.

My fascination had elbowed its way past my fear, at least until I heard the next command boom into my deaf ear and I nearly jumped out of my skin.

"GO TO YOUR LIVING ROOM AND SIT ON THE COUCH."

Can it hear my thoughts? I wondered as I dashed into the living room and sat on the sofa. It never occurred to me to disobey.

The Voice had used the word couch. Well, now I knew that it wasn't a New Yorker or it would have said sofa. *I bet He's not even Jewish*, I thought to myself. But what was I even thinking? HE!? How did I know it was a HE? It could be a ghost, a dybbuk, a Jewish wandering soul, pretending to be G-d.

"STEPHEN ZUCKERMAN, ARE YOU A GOOD PERSON?"

I was taken aback. It was said more like an accusation than a question.

"Well...yes, I think I am," I answered, even though I secretly didn't think I was.

"WHY? WHAT'S SO GOOD ABOUT YOU?"

I hesitated for only a second, but then went into automatic-mode, rattling off a litany of good deeds I'd done in my life, a catalogue I had no trouble recalling.

"Well, I'm a doctor, and I make a point of practicing with compassion and empathy, even if some of my patients are nasty, thankless low-lives." I continued, telling The Voice about when I returned money that was accidentally given to me by a store clerk. I voluntarily confessed to cheating on a big test, a confession that could have gotten me tossed out of the medical school, even though it was unlikely I would have been caught. I'd always gone out of my way to help relatives: my father almost died from urinary obstruction when his urologist missed the obstruction, but I caught it. An uncle couldn't swallow his food and his gastroenterologist blew the diagnosis. My uncle was starving to death, but I saved his life.

"EVIL…," The Voice murmured.

A chill ran through me to the bone. Evil? Me? I'd never associated that word with myself. I could be a jerk at times, like everyone else, but evil?

"EVIL...," The Voice repeated as if to underline my thoughts. "EVIL...," it said even louder. I started to sweat, but decided to power through my litany.

"When my Aunt Ethel had a disastrous hemorrhagic stroke, her children, my cousins, asked me to give an opinion—"

"EVIL...EVIL...EVIL...," The Voice kept repeating, cutting right through me now. I stopped abruptly, like a man about to walk off a cliff.

Could I really be evil? I asked myself. *What don't I know about myself?* The sofa was suddenly too uncomfortable. I fidgeted around but couldn't seem to relax. I felt like a bug pinned to a blotter. How was I going to get out of this mess? Obviously, this voice knows something about me. Maybe a lot about me.

Jews aren't very big on confession—not like the Catholics—but at least once a year, on Yom Kipper, we take an inventory of ourselves and promise to atone for our sins and shortcomings, so it's not entirely alien to us either. Even though I wasn't religious, I actually did observe the major Jewish holy days, so I had some concept of what was necessary here. Suddenly I knew what I had to do. *Okay*, I said to myself, *vomit it all up. Tell this voice all the evil you've done in your life.*

Tentatively, I started on an inventory of my faults. Without much effort, all the bad things I'd ever done came pouring out of me. Things I hadn't thought of in years, at least consciously, popped into my mind so readily that I realized I had been unconsciously carrying around that guilt. I talked about my first serious girlfriend, Myra Gluck, who had been 17-years-old when I dated her. I gave her my Stuyvesant High School Arista pin so she would think I cared for her, but what I really cared about was spreading her legs so I could finger her warm, wet pussy while we made out on the couch in her parent's basement. One drunken night stood out in my memory. At the water's edge on Rockaway Beach, I screwed her for the first time. Afterwards, she took me home to her parentless house, lovingly washed the sand off my naked body and put me to bed, snuggling up to me all night. I left for college the next week without even saying goodbye.

Then my parents came to mind. "I took everything my parents ever offered me and I never thanked them," I told The Voice. "They paid money they could hardly afford so that I could go to Union College in

Schenectady, New York. Of course I had to go to a private college, a less expensive public college would never do....

"And what did I do with their sacrifice? I squandered away my entire freshman year playing poker every night and sleeping through class during the day. Not once, ever, did they mention the financial sacrifices they had made for me, and as if I was entitled like a little prince, I took everything they offered without feeling I owed them anything, including gratitude.

"Yes, yes. You're right. I am evil." I felt the air being squeezed out of me. But I couldn't stop there—I had to tell all. I don't know how long I droned on about my various depravities, immoralities, debaucheries, and turpitudes, but eventually the words petered out. So did the anxiety I had felt at being exposed. I stopped.

As the words slowly faded, a sob escaped from my throat that shook my entire body. Then another, and another, and another until I could hardly catch my breath. Snot streamed down over my lips, mixed with my tears and I gasped for air as the sobs kept coming. Finally, I heard The Voice again.

"YOU'RE HUMAN…JUST HUMAN. MAYBE NOT THE BEST HUMAN BEING IN THE WORLD—FAR FROM IT. YOU'RE ARROGANT, SELF-CENTERED, INSENSITIVE, EGOISTIC AT TIMES, BUT YOU'RE NOT THE WORST HUMAN BEING IN THE WORLD, EITHER."

This was such a relief to hear. I cried for a long time until I finally exhaled a breath I'd been holding for far too long. That steadied me. I felt light. Even my body felt lighter. I had not realized how much guilt and shame I'd carried around with me all these years.

I felt a new quiet. I felt humbled. There was a blessed, warm stillness that seemed to wrap around me and cling. There was nothing more that night from The Voice, but for those moments I allowed myself to float in the weightlessness.

"I am free," I said quietly.

Okay, maybe "free" was a stretch, but I felt freer than I'd ever felt before.

Chapter 3: The Second Day

The next morning everything was eerily normal, as if The Voice had never been there at all. But all day it occupied my thoughts.

Is it here right now? I wondered as I stood very still in the middle of my kitchen, trying to sense its presence. But nothing happened. Maybe that was it. Maybe I'd never hear it again. Or maybe I dreamt it? No. It was real. More real than anything I'd ever experienced in my life.

Truthfully? I actually missed it. I mean, I really missed it. Like a lover, I missed it. Like a new lover, I yearned for it. All day long, I walked around exhilarated from the previous evening's mind-blowing events, like a boy with a bad case of first love. I became convinced that it would come again only at night. Hope stuck to me like a jungle sweat, and when I was done with my workday, I rushed home.

Without preliminaries, The Voice opened the conversation as soon as I walked through my front door.

"STEPHEN ZUCKERMAN, I HAVE COME TO TELL YOU THAT YOU ARE JESUS CHRIST RETURNED TO SAVE THE WORLD."

My first reaction was to laugh out loud. *What? What did The Voice say?* As these words settled in my deaf ear, I must have actually gaped at the empty air around me.

"Excuse me?" I said to the air.

"YOU ARE JESUS CHRIST AND YOU ARE HERE TO SAVE THE WORLD."

Chas v'chalila! G-d forbid! This thing is insane. Or am I the one who's nuts?

I burst out laughing again. "Really?! Jesus?" The very name Jesus was a cuss word to me, as it was to any Jew. What Jewish person would ever want to be Jesus?

"Jesus—the guy who's been hanging on crosses for a couple of millennium? That guy? The one in whose name millions of Jews, who shared my Yiddishkeit DNA back to Abraham and Isaac, have been tortured for the past two thousand years? That Jesus? Is that the guy you're talking about?"

Since childhood, the name Jesus sent shivers down my spine. By the age of five, I knew this guy was trouble. In the chador, we were taught never to mention his name.

Still, I was vaguely aware of the story of Jesus as told by the Christian gospels. The Voice began again.

"YOU ARE A HUNDRED PERCENT JEWISH—JUST LIKE JESUS WAS."

I confess, in all of my higher education, I never realized that Christians knew that Jesus had been a Jew. I'd never read the New Testament, and it had been a couple of lifetimes since I'd read the Torah. Even that I would have gladly skipped if I hadn't been forced to do so for my bar mitzvah. Reading it had the opposite effect than my Rabbi would have wanted; on the day of my bar mitzvah at thirteen, I stopped going to synagogue. I knew that Christians were waiting for Jesus to rise again but I didn't know why—maybe he didn't get it right the first time?—I just knew it was a big deal to them. In contrast, we Jews were still waiting for the messiah to show up for the first time.

"He'd have to come back as a thoroughbred Jew to get my attention," I mused, until it occurred to me that if this voice was actually G-d, it could hear my thoughts. Still, I somehow sensed that we'd already established an unspoken boundary, and that The Voice would respect my thoughts as private. Actually, it was only when The Voice chose to communicate with me that it seemed to hear my thoughts at all.

I continued chewing on these outrageous thoughts, and finally I said, "Seriously, the whole Jesus story has got to be a myth. The Immaculate Conception? Right. I'm a physician, don't forget. Walking on water? Resurrecting the dead? Please. How can any sensible, halfway intelligent person believe this is anything but fable?"

The Voice boomed out in my ear: "YOU ARE JESUS CHRIST RETURNED TO SAVE THE WORLD.

"Well, if I am," I retorted, "we'll have to renegotiate the crucifixion. And I prefer less celibacy and more boom-boom."

There was no response. The Voice clearly didn't think I was amusing. But I'd gotten away with that last bit of irreverence so I decided to keep it up.

"And, as long as we're on the subject, I'd like to die from a massive coronary in my sleep at about eighty-two."

Suddenly, I remembered back to when I worked at Community Mercy Hospital in Onamia, Minnesota about twenty years earlier. The hospital was run by the Franciscan nuns out of Little Falls, Minnesota, and two of the nuns had said that I looked like Christ. I was thirty-two at the time, with long hair and a beard, obviously Jewish, and doing missionary medical work. I had teased them by begging them not to hang me up on the cross in the front entryway, and it had made them laugh.

The Voice interrupted my thoughts.

"STEPHEN ZUCKERMAN, YOU ARE JESUS CHRIST, RETURNED. I DO NOT MAKE MISTAKES."

Why was The Voice taunting me again and again with this Jesus thing? Who wouldn't want to be world famous for doing good deeds and have the whole world (excluding some Jews), love him? *But wait. What am I thinking? Was I actually taking this seriously? As if I could be Jesus come back to save the world?!*

I was born in 1941 in Williamsburg—Jewish Brooklyn. Jesus's name was never mentioned by my parents or any relatives except maybe in a curse. Jesus followers went to church every Sunday and though my grandfather's synagogue in Williamsburg was a converted church, I feared going into other churches attended by Christians. Growing up, there was always tension between the Christian and Jewish communities. I even heard stories about Jews being accused of making Passover matzo using the blood of abducted Christian children. How ridiculous—matzo is off white, not red!

In the orthodox *chaders* and yeshivas (where I received what little Jewish education I had), Jesus was assumed to be one of the many false messiahs that the Torah warned against. The very fact that Jesus claimed to be "the son of G-d" ran counter to the very fundamental tenants of Judaism, as I understood it. G-d was the 'one and only.' Sure, there were claims that Jesus was a rabbi, that he was a reformer. But not G-d. As a child in yeshiva we were forbidden even from clasping our hands together and interlocking our fingers, because our thumbs would make the sign of the cross. We learned to put the fingers of one hand inside the fingers of the other, on our desk, to show obedience to our teacher. Even to this day, I don't interlock the fingers of my hands because it seems so wrong.

"Look, I can't be Jesus," I said to The Voice. "You're just messing with me. I'm not special. There are so many others who are more intelligent, like Albert Einstein. People who have achieved more and continue to achieve more. Great humanitarians like Mother Teresa and Albert Schweitzer who don't have half of my faults. I'm not a leader, a builder of empires, a philanthropist or the president of the USA. I don't go to synagogue or donate to Jewish causes. I might fit into the top ten percent in intelligence, but I was never able to pursue knowledge in depth, never able to become a professor or a scientist. I'm just an ordinary Jew."

On and on I went about why I couldn't be Jesus. But The Voice was just as relentless in its attempt to get me to believe I was Jesus.

Now, it's well known that Jews love to argue. Ask five Jews a question and you'll get six different opinions—and they'll argue until dawn about who is right. Why do you think Israel doesn't have a constitution? Nobody can agree. Not only can you not get a consensus from us about anything, but the innate urge to question authority is embedded into all Jewish children from birth. If I had to sum up Judaism in one sentence it would be: "Think for yourself, schmuck!"

What stuck from my Talmud years was that Jews have a long history of arguing with G-d. From Jacob who wrestled with an angel, to Moses who argues with G-d about destroying the People of Israel (and who, by the way, wins the argument), to Abraham who *hondles* with G-d over how many righteous men would justify saving Sodom and Gomorrah. It's a deeply embedded tradition never to accept something just because someone else says it is true, but to question, question, question until the knowledge becomes your own. I love the joke that illustrates this point:

Four Rabbis were arguing a point of doctrine and three of them agreed while the fourth strongly disagreed. Finally, the three Rabbis said, "If you disagree so strongly, why don't you ask God?" So, the dissenting Rabbi raised his hands to the heavens and began to speak. Suddenly the sun burned through the clouds and wreathed him in golden radiance, a heavenly chorus began to sing, and a great voice thundered from the heavens, **"HE IS RIGHT."** The three Rabbis looked up at the heavens, shrugged and said, "It's still three to two against you."

This tradition and practice has always marked independent thinkers who

cannot be led blindly like sheep, who think for themselves and who are genetically confident that they have the right to question even G-d. After all, why else would He have given humans intellect?

The night's conversation ended with me still stunned by The Voice's sudden

declaration. By claiming I was Jesus, I thought The Voice had shocked me as much

as it could. But I was clearly unprepared for what would happen the next evening.

Chapter 4: The Third Day

"YOU ARE G-D, STEPHEN ZUCKERMAN, AND YOU WILL CHANGE THE WHOLE UNIVERSE," The Voice told me the next evening.

I'd been skeptical about the proposition that I was Jesus, but this one sent me into a panic, flip-flopping between the certainty that I really had lost my mind and the consideration of the proposal.

With five billion other schlemiels on this planet, how could I be G-d Almighty? I'm not particularly good. I haven't fed the hungry masses, influenced world leaders to end wars, or changed world history. I have done next to nothing. It just doesn't fit together.

By then, I definitely believed The Voice was supernatural. What if it really *was* G-d talking? Why would He/It choose me? Was I to be next up? Maybe there was some larger plan at work here. I found the Yiddish word for 'Oh G-d!' rolling around in my head: *Gottenyu!*

I let myself consider the possibility. What a bonanza that would be! The look on my ex-wife's face when she found out that she'd been married to G-d made me burst out laughing. Then I thought about my kids. They'd certainly be proud of their dad's new role. People would talk about me forever. I'd never be forgotten. I'd spread wisdom throughout the world. You can't get more famous than G-d, can you? I chuckled to myself for a moment, but then quickly shook my head.

What was wrong with me? I couldn't believe I was actually considering the possibility.

But what if I was him.... *Hell, man, will you get a grip on yourself?* Then The Voice interrupted me.

"YOU ARE G-D, STEPHEN ZUCKERMAN. YOU WILL CHANGE THE UNIVERSE."

"No! No! No! No, I'm not!" I screamed back at it. "Is this some kind of trick? I couldn't possibly be G-d!? No human being can! And even if one of us could be, it wouldn't be this bupkis, this worthless, nothing person. There are others far more worthy!"

"IT'S JUST A JOB."

"What?"

"LIKE I SAID, IT'S A JOB. SOMEONE HAS TO DO IT. YOU JUST NEED TO BE A GOOD HUMAN BEING."

"That's it? A good human being? That's all? To be G-d?"

"THAT'S IT."

I began to think. Maybe I COULD be G-d. It means I could change a lot of things. I let my imagination begin to wander over the possibilities. I could stop wars. Images of the patients I'd treated over the years—especially the ones I'd felt the most helpless to save—filtered through my thoughts. I could get rid of diseases. Hell, I could get rid of poverty for that matter.

After a time of indulging those do-good fantasies, I realized that I could help myself, too. I could be the richest man on earth. I could make anyone do what I wanted. I could even have any woman I wanted. The possibilities were endless. I could go anywhere, even into people's heads. Stop hurricanes or start earthquakes. People would worship me. I'd make the Pope look like chopped liver!

But suddenly I had a different view of how my kids and friends would see me. How could Josh or Gabby ever treat me like "Dad" if I was G-d? I'd be put up on a pedestal by everyone. A sudden overpowering loneliness enveloped me, so empty that it felt like death.

That kind of power would make it impossible to have an easy familiarity with my children. No farting in the same room. No showing up at the breakfast table disheveled and still in a dream. No sitting in the same room reading and not talking. No taking anything for granted. Suddenly, those mundane things felt precious. The small, pedestrian comforts no one bothers to be grateful for suddenly appeared more essential than I'd ever realized. My kids couldn't look at me and relax, knowing they were home. I wouldn't be part of the wallpaper, like when they're obsessed with teenage things and ignoring my existence. They wouldn't feel a sense of security without ever needing to know why. They'd be self-conscious around me. On their best behavior. These thoughts made me even lonelier.

And what of my friends and colleagues? Who could ever be personal with me if I was G-d? If I stood above other human beings? Who would love me just for being me?

I was confused. I fretted. I paced. Eventually, I considered what an awesome responsibility it would be.

What a heavy load it would be to carry. How could I ever be sure I was doing the perfectly right thing?

Years ago, I'd met a famous guy and was struck at how people suddenly changed when he walked into the room, approaching him with reverence and awe. I realized how lonely fame must be. How could you just be yourself if people put you on a pedestal to adore you? As much as I wanted to be admired and recognized for my talents, the price of that admiration seemed too high. And if you showed the slightest sign of human weakness, they'd all say, "off with his head."

Then I understood why some people who win the lottery keep it a secret—it's the kind of thing that changes your relationship with everyone forever. You become a potential mark for anyone. Even if they didn't want something from you, how could you be sure? How would you know anyone loved you just for being you? I suddenly saw how a person could become an object, not a person. Who could you trust? Where would you go if you needed something? If you screwed up? If you let people down? I had never seen the advantage of being just a little *pisher*, a squirt, a nobody. It had never occurred to me that I might actually have more freedom than the rich, beautiful, or famous.

I don't think I'd like to be G-d after all. Not unless everyone else could be G-d, too! Had I misinterpreted The Voice's meaning when it declared that I was G-d, or was The Voice "playing" with me? To be G-d almighty must be awfully lonely. Maybe G-d is in all of us. Maybe I am G-d because G-d is in me; G-d is in all humans and to accept that is to never be lonely. I felt a growing joy creep up my body at this revelation. I am happy just being me, Dr. Zuckerman, Josh & Gabby's dad. That's plenty for me.

As the thought washed over me, I found myself weeping.

Chapter 5: The Spoken Word

The Voice didn't beat around the bush. None of our three nightly encounters had lasted more than half an hour, but the impact of those sessions roiled my brain. It was all I could think about—my secret companion. Wondering when The Voice would speak to me next. What would be up next for revelation? I both feared and desired it, waiting with trepidation and excitement for the moment when I would hear it inside my ear once again.

For all practical purposes, I was living alone. My wife of fifteen years had left me ten years before. Three years after that she finally let go, finally let me have a divorce. When she left our suburban rambler home, my son and daughter, twelve and fourteen years of age, stayed with me. Four years ago, my son moved out to live on his own; my daughter had already left the nest. Dick, a male friend of Madelaine's, my enigmatic girlfriend, rented my basement apartment, but I saw little of him. When home he preferred to drink his alcoholic thirst away in private.

Over the past few years, single life had become routinized. I was living in a house, but was someone who had no interest in doing so or skill in maintaining it. My early years were spent living as an apartment dweller in Williamsburg, Brooklyn. My father may have owned a hammer, but I never saw him use one.

My relationship with Madelaine was stranded, as routinized as the rest of my life; once a week we'd dine out at restaurants chosen by Madelaine, usually a neighborhood Perkins. Over chow, she incessantly picked my scientific brain with her intense curiosity. The evening ended with a sexual encounter at Madelaine's rented house, which almost always led to—at least me—having an orgasm. A payoff of sorts.

The fourth morning after The Voice's appearance, the day started as usual. Make the bed, do the wash, inventory the fridge and kitchen shelves, make a shopping list, take the garbage out. The same old routine, but now performed with a new awareness, a new excitement.

As I went about my mundane chores, I pondered the idea of The Voice. Tell others about it? Not a chance. For sure they would label me "crazy," and a part of me wanted to agree. But The Voice was right on the money, whacking away at my airs of superiority and inferiority, making me middle-of-the-road human. Its message was undeniable, and I, despite all my rationality, felt myself starting to give in to it. How could I deny its "stabbing at the heart" theater? This voice was some playwright and I wanted more show time.

Did this same voice speak to all humans, inspiring the Greek playwrights, leading Freud to psychoanalysis, Einstein to relativity? Did it speak to Abraham and Moses? Buddha, Joan of Arc? Were all great men and women tuned into their own personal version of The Voice, open to its loving truths? Did they act on those truths? I was a mere mortal; who was I to ignore this message? The Voice was allowing me to come face-to-face with myself. And maybe even with G-d.

I could not stay in my home and philosophize forever; the "real," the material world beckoned. The shriveled remnant of a Katz's delicatessen hard salami that I bought in New York four weeks before, plus mustard heavily spiked with horseradish, was applied to two slices of kosher rye bread to make my breakfast's barely chewable centerpiece. Then I went to the bathroom to prepare for business time, a board of director's meeting. Good stream, good aim, not a drop of urine outside the toilet bowl target. I combed my hair, plastering it down with tap water, never a gel or cream. I trimmed my beard, found clean trousers and a shirt, socks, my shoes, while all the while The Voice danced about in the back of my brain. I could hear it now, just on the edge of my thoughts. It was always with me, I realized, and that thought no longer scared me, but elated me.

Chapter 6: The Slime Mold

In the afternoon of day four, I was in the midst of a board meeting of HDII when I heard The Voice again.

"LET ME TAKE OVER," it said.

I sat in my chair, frozen, staring at the faces of the men around me.

HDII was a company I had founded in 1988 with Dr. Sid Stein, Chief of Cardiology at the University of Minnesota. I was chairman of the board. Sid and I were buddies, playing singles tennis together and socializing often over the years. HDII was his brainchild, aimed at revolutionizing the diagnosis of hypertension through dynamic analyses of the descending limb of the blood pressure wave-form. Arterial elasticity was the issue and HDII's technology was a paradigm shift ahead of static systolic and diastolic pressure measurements of assessing who did and who didn't have stiff arteries, hypertension.

I was in the prime of my venture capital years and had always been amazed that such a primitive and inaccurate 100-year-old technology—the blood pressure cuff—dominated the single largest medical condition that humans suffered from. Sid's vision tickled my venture capital brain cells. Here was the fuel to ignite a blockbuster venture deal, one that with Sid's reputation and the potential size of the market should be a snap to raise money for. If we succeeded it was guaranteed to give us hero status, maybe a Nobel Prize, transforming medicine in a big way.

The board meeting was being held in the University of Minnesota's cardiology department's conference room. At the time, the company was struggling to transform itself from a research/concept company into a manufacturing and marketing company.

The line-up of board members attending the meeting set the stage for drama. Included were:

Lawrence Frankel, PhD, veterinarian, was HDII's CEO. Larry was a master of FDA regulatory rules. He could write uplifting scientific diatribes that brought tears to my eyes. Larry had the temperament of a shy rhinoceros and the thick neck of one, too. You never knew if he was going to rush off and hide in the bush or, head down and horns up, barge full steam at you.

Harold Jester was a product of the Medtronic School of medical technology and creativeness, and a believer in angels. He claimed that as a child of ten, an angel had saved his life when he fell through the ice of a frozen river on a dark evening in rural, southern Minnesota. As he frantically searched for an opening in the ice, he realized he was going to die. Then he saw a light shining through the freezing water, and in a dreamlike state he followed it to a hole in the ice through which he could escape. When he emerged, the light was in the hand of a woman dressed in white who then led him home.

Harold was a brilliant conceptualizer who could enthrall investors with his vision. He packaged new product concepts into mouthwatering sales numbers to be achieved over a three to five year growth period. If Harold had a weakness it appeared to be his losing interest once he had helped to launch a company. He came across as a quarter horse in mile races. Harold was a student of neuro-linguistic programming. When in his presence I was always on the alert for NLP "manipulation," something I found to be great sport. If Harold were diminished twenty-five percent in size, he would have been my doppelgänger.

Mark Dinnock claimed to have been born with the "killer instinct." In order to avoid becoming a serial killer he took up martial arts as a youth and later joined the marine corps. Eventually, he got a PhD in physics and entered the world of medical technology. His spiritual world bristled with opportunistic alien forces that could penetrate the human skull and "invade" brains, for good and evil purposes. On the one hand, Mark could be concerned with launching a company aimed at preserving decorative flowers through better chemistry, and on the other he was knitted into a universe full of thought beams and transcendental activity.

My partner, Sid, was a researcher's researcher. He had a respect for the past, feet in the present, and a vision for the future of his field. He also had a love of publicity and that rare researcher's knack for simplifying complex medical concepts in order to make them digestible by "the lay community," without sounding patronizing. His cardiological fame spanned our globe.

Attending the HDII's board meeting—aside from the usual members—was a guest, a young lady who claimed expertise in technology that could help HDII gather blood pressure wave-form signals without having to insert catheters into arteries. The Voice bristled at her presence.

"LET ME TAKE OVER. I WANT TO QUESTION THIS LADY."

The hostile nature of the request struck me with alarm. Should I release The Voice? What was it up to? Would it create a fracas that I would obviously be blamed for?

To my surprise, my fear and trepidation morphed into a wave of excitement. *Unleash The Voice!* I thought. *Let this brilliance run rabid if that's what it wants to do.*

"ARE YOU STILL AFFILIATED WITH COMPANY X?" The Voice interrogated the young lady. I now knew The Voice could take me over if I agreed, could speak through me as if I was only a vessel. It was my voice, my body, but I was no longer the one doing the talking.

Shook up by The Voice's accusatory tone, the young woman hesitantly answered, "Well, yes, but I am not representing them at this meeting. I'm acting on my own as a consultant."

"WHY DIDN'T YOU TELL US OF YOUR CONFLICT OF INTEREST INSTEAD OF ME HAVING TO BEAT IT OUT

OF YOU? ARE YOU OUT TO STEAL CORPORATE SECRETS?" The Voice threatened.

Silence followed. The woman was flustered and embarrassed and did not say another word as she got up and left the meeting.

I could feel The Voice gloating inside of me; it was proud of scaring the lady away!

I thought that would be it, but then The Voice really put me on the line. It turned to the other board members.

"DO YOU BELIEVE THAT I AM G-D? THAT ALL OF YOU ARE G-D? THAT YOU HAVE G-D IN YOU?"

Harold and Mark were "believers," and they quickly exchanged glances.

"Yes, we know that's true," Harold said, answering for himself and Mark.

Sid and Larry were clearly shocked, glancing from each other to the rest of us, their mouths hung wide open. They did not know what to say, and being outnumbered three to two, they adjourned the meeting and beat a hasty retreat.

After that the meeting was over quickly. Mark and Harold were giving me significant looks, but I left the room in a trance, wondering what The Voice had done, and what would follow from its performance.

It was in the hallway that Mark and Harold caught up with me.

"Have dinner with us," Harold suggested. "We need to talk more about what happened at the meeting today."

"Alright," I agreed, sensing that they had something very important and encouraging to say. After all, they had agreed with The Voice. Hadn't they?

The setting of the restaurant reminded me of *My Dinner With Andre*. The lights were low, the tables mostly empty. We sat in a shadowy corner under a large painting of a fruit bowl.

"What's going on in your life?" Mark asked after we exchanged pleasantries.

"I have been visited by a voice," I explained, a little surprised at how free and comfortable I felt talking about my experiences. "I don't know what or who The Voice is, but it's taking me on some kind of journey and I'm a willing and excited traveler."

The two men did not look horrified, so I continued. "This Voice claims that we humans are G-d. Not G-d

Almighty, but the embodiment of love. The more we express that love, the more we express the G-d in us. By expressing love we influence those around us who are open to the "love beams" to also express their love, spreading, it to others ad infinitum, changing the whole universe."

Mark and Harold's expressions signaled approval and understanding of what I had expressed. Then Mark told of his own beliefs. "There are energy beams streaming through the universe that are capable of entering our brains and then depositing knowledge of the universe into the open mind. Once the open mind receives this knowledge, it can spread it to other open minds. Have you ever heard of the slime mold, Stephen?"

"Never, I'm sure. I wouldn't be quick to forget a nasty name like that," I replied.

"You know about amoebas?" Mark asked.

I nodded. Amoebas are favorites of high school biology teachers, the building blocks of the multi-cellular animal world—us included. They do it all: eat, defecate, sense light, gravity and pH, and live eternally by dividing in half to propagate. I even spied one once under the microscope conjugating, having sex! H.G. Wells wrote a story about a scientist who falls in love with a creature he discovers in a drop of water under his microscope, most likely an amoeba. I told Mark the story, including the tragic ending: the drop of water that makes up the creature's microscopic world inadvertently dries up to the scientist's great dismay.

"Well," Mark said, "there is another side, if you will, to the amoeba's life. When the amoeba's world is threatened by a hostile environment—a change in pH, a decreasing water supply, you name it—one amoeba will begin to secrete a chemical substance in greater quantity than usual. This substance causes a major chain-reaction in all the amoebas in chemical shot of the original amoeba. That amoeba becomes known as the head amoeba. In response, the rest of the amoebas also begin secreting larger quantities of this mysterious chemical and start swarming about the head amoeba. Eventually, thousands of amoebas can become involved in the swarm and then, most miraculously, the swarm fuses itself into a larger, multi-nucleated creature—the slime mold."

Mark's description of the evolution of the slime mold caused an immediate cascade of thoughts to resound through my brain. Was this the story of transformation, of how I, G-d, and others would change the universe? It reminded me of The Voice, of G-d being awakened in each amoeba by a chemical love transmitter that changed the amoebas' very universe.

I spent the next morning at the UMN medical library researching the slime mold. I was trembling with anticipation of what I might find. It was as though G-d, the cosmic force propelling the universe, was to be revealed to me.

The story of the amoebas' transformation into the slime mold was prophetic, one studied by legions of biologists and social anthropologists. This is where The Voice wanted me to go, I thought. I dove into my research, expanding on what Mark had told me the night before.

When the head amoeba, or amoebas—there could be more than one head—was affected by a noxious change in environment, it was stimulated to secrete cyclic amp in larger quantities than other amoeba. Any amoeba in contact with this increased outpouring of cyclic amp, or the love chemical, also increased their secretion of cyclic amp to the point where it equaled that of the head amoeba(s). This caused all the stimulated amoebas to join together and give up their individual identities in order to create a new egalitarian society: the slime mold! The head amoeba(s) acted to save its fellow amoebas as they sensed their world was endangered. The slime mold was the "voluntary" uniting of amoebas in a way to better deal with the environmental stress that the head amoeba(s) sensed. Individual amoebas did not totally lose their identity; rather they gave up their cell membrane but kept their nuclei's identity, their core.

When the slime mold itself felt threatened, it produced cysts, sealed capsules filled with nuclear material. When a nourishing environment again appeared, the cysts would burst open, egg-like, and deliver a whole new generation of amoeba.

The process immediately spoke to me; the universal society of humans portrayed by a slime mold? Nirvana where all souls are drops in one sea. No longer separate entities, but not totally absorbed into one being. Still individual amoeba nuclei, but moving within one slime skin! It was what I envisioned for this world: release of the individual amoeba-self in order to be as one with its fellow amoeba nuclei in the slime mold's bag of protoplasmic soup. I left the university library with my brain a-swim, hardly able to avoid street traffic as I contemplated what this all meant.

Chapter 7: The Plot Thickens

The day after my awakening to the life of the slime mold, The Voice struck again. A corporate board meeting was once again the setting, though this time the company was Image Premastering Services (IPS). Again, I was the chairman of the board, the center of gravity for the company. Again, the willful and threatening Voice spoke into my deaf ear, directly into my brain.

"LET ME TAKE OVER."

Oh Lord, here we go again, I thought. I knew The Voice was going to say what I wouldn't dare to. Because of that, I hesitated, but deep inside I knew I wanted this supernatural force, this super-mind within me to speak out. Like my last ride on Coney Island's Cyclone roller coaster, I took a deep breath and prepared for sweet terror.

"CLARK, YOU ARE CONSPIRING WITH THE CHINESE TO STEAL OUR TECHNOLOGY, TRUE OR FALSE?" The Voice said accusingly.

"I don't understand," Clark sputtered. The other board members were stunned into silence.

"STOP THE BULLSHIT, YES OR NO?" The Voice shouted menacingly.

Again, Clark tried to defend himself. But The Voice barred his every arguable escape route.

"I don't have to answer this," Clark finally said. He stood up and fled from the meeting.

The Voice commanded me to follow Clark out to his car, where I accused him again. For a moment, I worried I might get beat up. Clark was a former Williams College football player and still broad-shouldered and strong. But instead of punching me out, Clark shrank hastily into his low-slung sports car and screeched away, leaving me in a cloud of white exhaust.

I stood in the parking lot, watching him leave, wondering what The Voice's motive was. It was ridiculous to think that Clark was selling our technology to a competitor, let alone a Chinese competitor, so I assumed that The Voice knew it too. I wondered why it had chosen to create such a scene. It was only later that night, when I had the time to contemplate the situation, that I realized The Voice was trying to shake Clark up enough to get him out of his self-consciousness. He was normally closed, with a controlled, unshakeable demeanor that irritated the hell out of me. The Voice wanted him to reveal a part of himself to others, to me, to reveal to us all that he was a human being. No other accusation, made in a public setting, could have shaken him as much as this one did.

I realized The Voice was using me to affect some kind of radical change in a man who resisted radical changes in favor of an imposing order. Never mind that it made me look totally out of my mind, deluded, and psychotic. And I was aware of how I was being perceived, don't get me wrong. But I was beginning not to care anymore. The Voice was trying to deepen my relationships with the people around me, trying to put them out of their elements to enact some kind of personal growth in all of us. And how could that be a bad thing?

The next IPS board meeting was held in a hotel conference room in St. Louis Park. I'd been tipped off by another board member that the sole purpose of the meeting was to dislodge me as chairman. Surprisingly, I did not take this personally. With The Voice in my life, I was too distracted to care much about boardroom politics. I went to the meeting that day knowing there was a higher agenda. So I wasn't surprised when The Voice once again requested to take charge of me. Ignoring the political incorrectness of talking about "G-d" in normal business milieu, I let go of the reins of my behavior and let The Voice have its head.

"I AM G-D," The Voice, my voice, proclaimed. "WE ALL HAVE G-D IN US. DO YOU AGREE?" I looked from one member to the next, as if I was gathering a consensus. Everyone squirmed in their seats except the Jones brothers, our company techno-dreamer-wizards, who were, by nature, ever ready to consider the theoretical or spiritual nature of the universe. One of the brothers spoke up.

"Well, ah, yes. I think if there is a G-d, it's…He's probably inside of us as well as outside."

The other brother joined the conversation with ease, not at all nonplused about where this line of reasoning was headed. "Sure, he's inside of us—that's what we call our soul. Of course there is no actual scientific proof of the soul, but then, science's measuring stick has been proven to be, at best, limited."

He adjusted himself in his seat and seemed to settle in to wait and see where this was going.

The first brother added, "Inside, outside—those are relative terms, since the matter inside one particle is surrounded by space and parts of ever increasing amounts of matter and space."

"SO IF G-D, IS INSIDE OF US, AS YOU SAY, THEN WE ARE PART OF HIM, RIGHT?" The Voice looked around for another victim to put on the spot, and was vaguely aware that people were starting to exchange looks. The Voice didn't care, only focused on another member. "RIGHT, JOHNSON?"

Johnson shrugged and said, "I suppose so...."

"SUPPOSE SO? DON'T YOU THINK ABOUT IT? ISN'T IT ONE OF THE MOST IMPORTANT THINGS IN THIS WORLD TO THINK ABOUT? OR IS IT ALL ABOUT MAKING MONEY?" The Voice demanded. It was right, of course. I started to lose my personal discomfort at being politically incorrect by talking G-d at a business meeting—much less one where my credibility was being questioned—and I fell in step with the game The Voice was playing. I found it enormously entertaining, making these guys squirm, not out of a sadistic humor, but because, by now, I knew that The Voice was usually up to something much bigger than I could imagine. So, I let it go on, discussing whether we were all G-d, who was G-d, and watched as everyone, eventually, bowed out of the room. Soon, The Voice and I were alone.

But not for long.

The squeak of leather drew my attention to the door of the conference room, which had been left open when the last board member fled. Filling the door were two very imposing police officers.

"Dr. Zuckerman, we're here to check on a problem," one of them explained, with the kind of deliberate calmness that they are taught to use when dealing with emotionally disturbed people. The Voice was suddenly courteous.

"NO PROBLEM, OFFICER. AS YOU CAN SEE, NOTHING HAS BEEN BROKEN, NO ONE WAS ASSAULTED. IT WAS JUST A DISAGREEMENT AMONG BOARD MEMBERS. NOTHING UNUSUAL FOR CORPORATE BOARD MEETINGS."

The police officers listened politely, looking around at the empty seats, but they weren't put off.

"Yes, we can see, everything looks to be okay here. Still, we would like to take you down to Hennepin County Hospital to make sure you're okay, too."

I knew they weren't really asking me to accompany them, they were demanding it. A refusal on my part would most likely cause them to use force.

"DON'T RESIST," The Voice advised me, and, of course, I obeyed. They didn't cuff me or even guide me out physically, since I went quietly with them. They put me in the back of their car without any controls for the door or the window, and drove me to the Emergency Room of Hennepin County Hospital. There, I was locked into a room where I was to wait for someone to appear and tell me what they were going to do with me. I was more curious than afraid or anxious. It seemed like just another stop on the very big adventure that I was on.

With its four bare walls and a voyeur's camera bolted into the crotch where ceiling met wall, the room was stark and cold. The Voice went silent and so, therefore, did I. After a few hours, my friend, Sid, and Laurie, Madelaine's daughter, came to vouch that I was perfectly harmless. I was released to their custody. I wanted to ask where Madelaine was, but I didn't, assuming she was too busy or too freaked out to come herself.

After my release, the three of us went to get coffee at a nearby tacky downtown restaurant. It was around 2 p.m. and no one was in the place other than us. Once again, The Voice took over, repeating its *G-D IN ME, G-D IN YOU, G-D IN ALL OF US*, theme. I started to suspect that Sid and Laurie weren't sure they'd done the right thing by bailing me out.

Two weeks later, The Voice pulled another "riot act" at a shareholders' meeting for a company called Black Hawk Holdings. The president of the company was revered by most everyone there, and he delivered a rousing "State of Black Hawk" speech that got a big applause. I felt my body being pulled into a standing position amidst all the shareholders. I began to head toward him, cornering him for confrontation.

The Voice pointed out his treachery to me, and insisted that I lay into him for his lying. It instructed me to accuse him of embezzling funds from the company.

My/our outburst, the huge accusation, upset everyone who was within earshot.

But, as insane as it must have seemed at the time, the accusations that The Voice made were apparently partly true. It's just that no one seemed to know it yet. The president was relieved of his duties a few weeks later.

Looking back, whenever The Voice asked to "take over" it was clearly an act of willing submission on my part to let go. Even knowing the havoc it could and did create in my name did not dissuade me from consenting, because The Voice astonished me with its brilliance. It knew things I didn't know. It revealed things I needed to have revealed, both to me and to the people around me. There was no doubt in my mind that I was experiencing a super intelligence. I, Stephen Zuckerman, could never have the amazing effect on others that The Voice was having. So even though I was hesitant, even though I knew I would be giving others the impression that I was crazy, when it spoke to me in my deaf ear and asked for permission to take over, I still yielded the floor to my voice.

Chapter 8: Psychiatry Enters, Stage Left

"Steve, I'd like you to meet a psychiatry buddy of mine over at the University." The fact that Sid and I are both Jewish, plus the psychiatrist's last name sounding more kosher than mine, made me assume he was Jewish too. Psychiatry with cultural undertones. *Freud be with you*, I thought. I also assumed my "outburst" at the HDII board meeting and my getting arrested at the Image Premastering board meeting was why Sid thought I needed to see a shrink.

"What's up, Sid? Do you think I'm crazy, that there isn't a G-d force in us?" I asked him. "Harold and Mark agree with me."

But Sid stuck to his guns and since The Voice made no suggestions, I agreed to the visit.

I don't like psychiatrists, or psychiatry. To me there is medicine and then there is pseudoscience: psychiatry. Nobody in all my extended family ever had a psych diagnosis, ever saw a shrink. There was however, one psychiatrist in the family, Joseph Reiss, my maternal great uncle Lionel Reiss's only child. Lionel, who trained as a commercial artist in his twenties, set out from New York City in the 1920s. He traveled to Eastern Europe, where his family had lived after their expulsion from Spain, to prove that the Jews living in *shtetls* there were a race unto themselves. Equipped with sketchpads and pencils, he pedaled his bicycle across Eastern Europe recording the faces of his people. His conclusion was there was no single Jewish race, a conclusion Hitler, a few years later, refuted with murderous intent. Lionel, acknowledged for his great European odyssey, was also my family's cultural and intellectual champion. He was also a hero to all Jews for having helped preserve images of those poor souls living in a world soon to be decimated. No matter how generous, how caring Lionel was to me—and he always was—I felt ashamed of myself in his presence.

Joseph, four years older than me, went to Harvard and trained there to be a psychiatrist. I never knew him personally, having spent maybe two hours in his presence in my entire life. While he became well known in his field of family psychiatry, my dim view of the discipline Freud had created clouded my acceptance of his achievements.

My distrust of psychiatry could in part be traced to Mt. Zion Hospital in San Francisco where I spent two years in medical residency in the late '60s. Mt. Zion was a hotbed of psychiatric training. We were in the bosom of the Fillmore District at the height of Haight. LSD, uppers and downers, marijuana, and psychiatry had infiltrated the hospital. Robert Wallerstein, a dominant figure in his field, was Chief of Psychiatry. At the time, I had a three-month rotation to spare in my internal medicine training program and I decided to give psychiatry a whirl.

Instead of enlightenment, I became even more jaded against the practice. The psych-residents all seemed obsessed with how others viewed them. At a round table discussion I noticed one resident intensely watching the twitches of another resident, while yet another observed him. *Who was watching me?* I regularly wondered.

While sitting on fold up chairs next to each other, one resident stretched his upper torso, putting his arm inadvertently around the chair next to him. The other resident jerked forward in his seat. Panicked by what I assume he felt could be taken as a personal gesture, the first resident quickly withdrew his arm. Both residents were male, as were almost all the others. Did the first resident fear his action would be misconstrued as a homosexual advance? Seemed that way to me. An inappropriately over-the-top reaction to a simple touch.

These guys were off balance, nuts. Psychiatry was for fruitcakes, I decided. The id, ego, super-ego, mesomorphs, ectomorphs, endomorphs—all gobbledygook! Give me pneumonia and penicillin, appendicitis and surgery, a heart attack. Something real.

Which is why I was wary when Sid suggested I see his "friend." The day of my appointment, he led the way through the bowels of the University, until we finally reached the office of his buddy. The deeper we walked into the inner sanctum, the more trapped I felt. Once we were in the psychiatrist's office, Dr. X came out to greet Sid and me. The Voice immediately spoke up in my deaf ear.

"SHAKE HIS HAND AND LEAVE. DO NOT TALK TO HIM," The Voice ordered. It carried such authority; I had no question about obeying this directive. Besides, I didn't need The Voice to convince me I didn't want to deal with Dr. X. When Sid introduced us I shook the shrink's hand, did an about-face and walked out of the office without explanation. I am sure that the expression on Sid's face was dismay, maybe even embarrassment, but it had no influence on me. I had my marching orders. I trusted and fully agreed with my commanding officer.

This was to be the first in a number of occasions where The Voice instructed me on how to deal with psychiatrists (who were about to become major players in my rapidly changing life). From the beginning, The Voice set out to trap them—to trap psychiatry itself by striking at its Achilles' heel.

Chapter 9: Meeting Madelaine (Captivated)

I met Madelaine in 1986, five years before The Voice first spoke to me. To this day, she remains an enigma. I dated her—a term that hardly fit our relationship—for some five years, but was never able to get a handle on who, exactly, she was. Madelaine had a workout-hardened body and at the same time was voluptuous; she was brilliant and dyslexic, occasionally spastic, a loner with a thousand friends in the political, art, business, and science communities in Minneapolis. She spoke of a secret self, a self that she felt driven to conceal and had done so except for rare "slip-ups."

I didn't really meet Madelaine; she met me. A female admirer of mine— actually a woman infatuated with me, probably in good part due to my lack of interest in her—invited me to a party, one with clearly sexual overtones, enough overtones to make me want to go, even with her. The party was to be a private happening at the Sheik's Palace Royale, a high-class strip joint in downtown Minneapolis. The co-sponsors, I was told, were Madelaine and Mike. The two had been lovers and amateur archeological adventurers in Israel and Central America. The party's theme was "ancient digs" and its purpose was to raise money for Madelaine and Mike to mount an archeological expedition to "somewhere or other."

None of the crowd resembled anyone from my inhibited medical world and many were in costumes that appeared straight out of an *Indiana Jones* movie. Feeling like a sore thumb, I convinced my date to retreat to the bar and play voyeurs. Suddenly, out of nowhere, came this raspy, deep-throated voice: "What's cooking, good looking?"

Is this corn aimed at me? I thought. There, situated between my date and I, dressed from head to toe in safari gear with brown knee-high leather boots, khaki short-shorts, and blouse open almost to her navel, stood Madelaine. Her strawberry blonde hair flowed out in all directions from under a pith helmet, her wide mouth surrounded by thick moist red lips and populated with a full set of brash white teeth. Her sun-bronzed skin was exposed everywhere, her torso was full of the right curves and led the eye toward her tauntingly exposed legs, ones that had an ever-so evocative subtle concavity at the outer aspect of her knees. Madelaine's sharp, squinty eyes focused on mine as she leaned into me. My woman friend evaporated.

Without any recollection of how we got there, we ended up heatedly entwined in each other in my VW bus parked in downtown traffic. *This was too good,* I thought, *Police, police stay away, come back another day!* Madelaine's educated tongue was down my throat. Somehow I managed to open her blouse and fondle her full breasts. Should I push the envelope? Madelaine's legs were open. She left no obstacle except her safari shorts and her underpants between my groping left hand and her twat. "Let's wait to screw next time," a heavily breathing Madelaine counseled. I had soaked my pants—and Madelaine knew it. I was smitten. "Okay," was about all I could muster.

Madelaine invited me to spend the next weekend with her at a farm cabin she was renting for the summer. The cabin was southwest of Pease, a tiny ethnic Dutch village—miniature windmills and all—on a stretch of Highway 169, seventy miles north of Minneapolis. The farm bordered the west branch of the Rum River. It was early summer and the bucolic stream, no wider than ten yards across, gurgled with newfound waters as it meandered through central Minnesota on its way to join the Rum River some thirty miles downstream. The Rum, in its turn, flowed into the Mississippi just north of Minneapolis and the two traveled south to New Orleans and the Gulf of Mexico, where they joined the oceans of the world.

That first afternoon in the kitchen of Madelaine's rented cabin, she, without notice, went down on her knees, opened my pants' zipper and proceeded with the endearing act of caressing my penis with her lips, her tongue, her mouth.

Madelaine was not alone on the farm. She had three cats that she cared for, and they in turn hunted down the local field mice that were having a field day in the unattended, well-watered, weed-infested fields. Madelaine seemed content in nature, occupied by tending her modest garden, cleaning house, mothering her cats, caring for me.

That first evening at the cabin Madelaine and I lay in bed holding each other. She snuggled her head into my neck. I felt her warm calm breath and the gentle heave of her chest.

The next day I waded into the shallows of the west branch of the Rum, fishing rod in hand, and cast from one shoreline to the other. Cautiously, I waded down the sunlit stream giving notice to all: "Ready or not, here I come!" A skittish northern pike confusingly darted between my legs, tickling the hairs of my calf; a bass took my lure and danced about me on the line. All the fish I caught that day were eventually set free, returned to their joyous existence in the cool, flowing stream waters.

Later that summer, Madelaine invited me to a party at an upscale high-rise overlooking Loring Park near downtown Minneapolis. The twenty-fourth floor apartment was being rented by a longtime friend, a woman Madelaine had shared many "wild adventures" with. Both were single, had broken marriages that included a child, and were sexually "free." Julia was a tall, brash, buxom bleached-blonde who worked in marketing for a country western music magazine. The party was loaded with denizens of the music industry.

I felt again like a fish out of water. A wannabe on land, finding it hard to breath. So I drank instead. Drunk as a skunk, Madelaine and I danced a tawdry, sensuous, unscripted dance, full of bumps and grinds and impassioned body contact—the best body contact since my rush hour New York subway days. Madelaine, in her best deep-throated voice, whispered moistly in my ear, "I know who you are."

Soon after the Bacchanalian dance, exhausted and drunk, I fell asleep on the floor in a corner of the apartment's living room. Much to my regret I was informed that during my snooze, Madelaine, Julia, and a third woman friend cavorted about the apartment dressed as lingerie models.

Chapter 10: The Halcyon Years

Madelaine: "I have to move out of my apartment by next Tuesday."

Me: "Why?"

Madelaine: "I'm two months behind on my rent."

Me: "What are you going to do?"

Madelaine: "I found a small house to rent near River Road—a darling house, and the owner is a friend of a friend and will give me a deal."

Me: "Oh, that sounds good."

Madelaine: "Well, yes, but I need to come up with a $300 security deposit."

Me: "Are you working?"

Madelaine: "Yes, I'm cashiering at this food co-op in the area. Very lovely people. The other cashier is a kid who I'm helping through a crisis. I had her over for dinner last night."

Me: "What about the cabin near Pease?"

Madelaine: "I stopped renting it."

Me: "How are you going to survive?"

Madelaine: "I'll see."

Me: "I can loan you the $300."

Madelaine: "Okay."

For the first four years of our relationship, Madelaine and I fell into a pattern that seemed to suit us both. Madelaine worked scatteringly, never quite earning enough to get by. Through her network of friends she received breaks on this or that and she received money from me when backed against the wall. We "dated" once a week. We had dinner together, usually at a Perkins in the neighborhood where her rented house was located. We would spend hours in the restaurant discussing mostly science, medicine, and business. Madelaine's mind was avidly curious and capable of comprehending a wide variety of concepts. She was like an eclectic sponge that never soaked up enough to be saturated.

After dinner, we would go to her rented house and she provided me with sex, making sure one way or another that I had an orgasm. I was never sure if Madelaine had one or not, or even if sex interested her. As for me, an orgasm served more than one purpose—

pleasure yes, but also prostatitis prevention. Regular sex, not masturbation, was the best prevention and treatment for a recurrent problem of mine. One time after sex, Madelaine surveyed my body; "Nice legs, not a bad tush," she said.

Eventually, Madelaine told me all about her heterosexual life and the well-founded fear she had of dying of the complications of her Crohn's disease. Crohn's nearly killed her and did cripple her for a while in her early twenties. Her breakups with men almost always led to an exacerbation of her disease. She made a rule to never remarry and, as well as possible, balance her need for long term security through monogamous relations—with a constant need for distance. I never knew how much Madelaine cared for me—or if she did at all—as her emotions always seemed masked, in part I am sure because I wanted them that way.

Madelaine knew artists, politicians, lawyers—the in-crowds. She volunteered her time to all sorts of causes, and introduced me to her band of movers and shakers.

"Meet Ari, he's an art professor at MCAD. He's doing experimental work with this media or that."

"Hi Ari, I'm Stephen. I'm a physician, but I'm doing venture capital right now," I said, feeling more like a philistine.

Madelaine was the one who introduced me to the Jones brothers, who had started a company that transferred museum quality images onto video discs. She'd helped them get the company off the ground. I helped fund them, and eventually became the company's chairman—all thanks to Madelaine.

Over the years I gained some insight into Madelaine's past. "When I came to Minneapolis, my Crohn's disease was so raging that I got severe Crohn's arthritis and had to walk with crutches. I was only twenty-two and had never before been away from Texas. I don't ever want to make my Crohn's come back; it would kill me the next time. That's why I won't ever get married again." At another time, Madelaine admitted her mother was an alcoholic. "If I drink, I'll become an alcoholic like her. Well, you're a doctor. You know what will happen to me. I'm scared shitless of whiskey." I rarely saw Madelaine with a drink. Marijuana was another story.

"My father disappeared when I was five or six. I mean disappeared into thin air. My mother told me that he had died, but there was no funeral, no burial! One day he was there, the next he was gone. No matter how hard I tried to find him, there were only dead ends. I think he must have worked for the CIA and they sucked up his identity."

Madelaine studied me like a carnivore studies its prey. I wasn't the only one she did this to. She had a need to dominate, to manipulate, and had the intellect and interest to do so. Her weak spot was her monstrous jealousy, which, if not kept at bay, would trigger her Crohn's disease. I know this because she told me so time and time again.

"What's wrong, Madelaine?" I queried her one day. We were visiting NYC and staying in my brother, Bob's, Greenwich Village studio apartment on 6th Avenue, right across the street from what was the New York Woman's House of Detention, now a community garden, and the Jefferson Market Library. Madelaine had huddled herself by the apartment's window. I was alarmed by how small and frightened she appeared. This wasn't the powerhouse I knew. After two or three hours she puffed up, returned to normal, never explaining what had happened.

During those seemingly halcyon years of our relationship, my venture capital world expanded almost manically. I had four paydays in all that time, but they were big enough to cover my bills and then some. Age fifty was coming. The rumblings in my brain, like the warning signs of an impending earthquake, had recently made themselves known, for the second time in my life.

The first time the dogs left Rabaul in 1937, no one took notice. Within weeks the surrounding volcanoes spewed forth ash that buried the town. Fifty-seven years later, the citizens of the rebuilt port understood what it meant when the dogs left town. Within days the volcanoes struck again. I was that town, and what was happening in my mind was equivalent to the dogs leaving. Still, what was I to do with this churning feeling that a volcano was once again about to burst?

Chapter 11: Joel Black Knife and The Mrs.

Madelaine spent six weeks every summer at the famous paleontologist, Jack Horner's, dinosaur dig in Montana. "*Madelaine, how can you volunteer and work for nothing for this guy, when you're broke and don't even have a job?*" was what I wanted to ask her. I didn't dare. While I was frustrated by her lack of responsibility, another part of me envied her constant freedom.

Madelaine's junker collapsed just prior to her leaving for the digs. She was frantic and let me know. I had been a customer at Westside Volkswagen for some twenty years. Only once had I bought outside the Volkswagen family of cars. For two years I owned a Saab Turbo. When the Turbo kicked in, so did I—caution went to the wind. The car plagued me with mechanical woes. I went back to Volkswagens.

I took Madelaine to Westside and the used car salesman dug up a '60s Beetle full of dings and rust, but with a sound heart and tires. I didn't mind buying Madelaine the car until she started muttering, loud enough for me to hear: "What a bastard, making me drive this ugly old junker." That pissed me off. I began thinking, *Oh, no you don't—you're not going to manipulate me this way.* And I dug in my metaphorical heels. Out of pure spite, I acted totally oblivious when she'd put on the pout.

I guess I won, because she gave up her campaign to get me to buy her a better car. I'm not sure that it ever occurred to her, either, that she could buy a better one herself if she got a job. But whatever her thinking on the subject, she eventually decided to drive the thing to Montana, grumbling all the way, I'm sure.

At about that time, I was serving on the board of a non-profit arts organization in Minneapolis called The Playwrights' Center. There I met Joel Black Knife, an Assiniboine playwright.

Joel, half-black and half-Indian, was the product of an Indian reservation horror show—incest, beatings, alcoholism. He was also, he said, a sober drunk, thanks to his wife.

His writing bit hard into white ignorance of life on an Indian reservation—in his case the Fort Peck Reservation in Montana—but in person he was gentle, with a subtle wit that immediately made me like him. I never got the impression that Joel was angry at white folks. If anything I think he was angry about his dysfunctional upbringing. I identified him as a transcultural figure—alienated from his tribal world and, while able to speak eloquently to the rest of America, he wasn't part of mainstream culture, either. Not so different than myself as a non-practicing Jew living in Christian-dominated Minnesota, only one generation removed from fervent public displays of anti-Semitism.

Joel's wife, who was white, was his opposite—perpetually pissed off at anyone who had an ounce of authority. She had the physique of a surly bear: dense, formidable, and dangerous. And, secretly, she scared the shit out of me.

As I got to know the Black Knifes, Mrs. Black Knife tirelessly chronicled her extensive shoulder, back, and neck pain from falling off ladders as a seasonal apple-picker or being in the wrong place as a logger. This was before I had much experience as a physician with chronic-pain patients and, privately, I doubted the legitimacy of her complaints. She was so thoroughly, so utterly, so relentlessly truculent that I grew to accept her in the same way that the mind stops noticing a constant, deafening roar.

Nonetheless, I found myself volunteering to accompany her to her disability hearing, primarily because I knew that with her cantankerous attitude, she had little-to-no chance of getting approved on her own. According to her, the physical ailments she claimed had rendered her unemployable. In truth, she could out-hike, out-lift, and out-climb me at every turn. But I had to be straight with her, and so, swallowing the terror she inspired in me, I told her: "I'll go with you to the hearing and testify as your doctor, but I want you to know that I can't, in good conscience, testify that your injuries have left you permanently *physically* disabled."

She scowled. "So what-the-fuck-good are you then?"

"Well, I can testify truthfully to one thing—that you're crazy," I paused, waiting for her fist to come out of nowhere and clock me, "and therefore, you are, indeed, unemployable."

She stared at me for a long moment as Joel quaked with silent laughter in the background. I got the impression he would have broken into shrieks of glee if she had tackled me right then and there. We both knew that the chances of this happening were greater than not. But I managed to stand my ground and hold her stare as I saw the wheels spinning in her head.

She turned her back, shrugged, and said, "Fuck if I care what you say, as long as I get the goddamned disability." So, we left it at that.

At her hearing, the judge and social worker questioned her, and it was clear that they were working very hard to appear empathetic. They jumped right in and asked her to describe her injuries, reassuring her with sympathetic expressions that they were well-practiced at donning.

As she began to speak, she let a loud sob escape, then melodramatically took a deep breath and continued, punctuating her story with sniffs and sputters through minutely detailed descriptions of what had happened to her and how she'd suffered. She so overplayed the victim role that I almost began to laugh at several points. The only thing that actually stopped me was that I knew, however flawed her presentation was, she really *had* suffered.

The judge and the social worker, barely able to stifle their yawns, nodded like benevolent puppets, making occasional notes when they couldn't look her in the face. They asked if she was still able to work, even though the answer was obviously no. Then, they asked how she had been supporting herself, up to the present, considering all the things she'd described. Suddenly, Mrs. Black Knife puffed up, changed character, and went on the attack.

"You *fucking* lazy-assed big shots sit around all day on your rear ends and then have the balls to ask me how I make it? Have you ever worked a day in your lives? And you look down on ME?! What the hell do you know about my pain and suffering? Oh, but you think you know, don't you? 'Cuz you know everything, you fucking elitist pigs!"

A resounding silence froze the air in the room as the judge and social worker blinked, blank-faced, trying to decide whether they had actually witnessed what they had actually witnessed. I hadn't seen such great entertainment in a long time. Finally, the air started moving again as the social worker spoke. "Yes, well, I think we can skip to the next step. Dr. Zuckerman? You are here to testify for Mrs. Black Knife, are you not?

"Yes, I am," I said as I stood up.

"Well, Mrs. Black Knife, you are very fortunate to have your personal physician come and testify. Most people are not that privileged."

"Fuck you, you self-righteous bitch," Mrs. Black Knife replied. "Why the hell wouldn't I have my doctor here?"

The judge rushed to quell any further outbursts by quickly addressing me. "Yes, yes, Dr. Zuckerman, would you please tell us about your patient here."

So I began. "The fact of the matter is that I am not actually convinced that Mrs. Black Knife's history of physical injuries limits her ability to work. She shows remarkable strength at times and maybe it's sheer willpower on her part, but I have seen that she is physically quite able to do any number of activities. Until medical science invents the Pain-O-Meter that can objectively measure an individual's pain, doctors will not be able to confirm that a person's pain is disabling. Even lousy looking x-rays of knees and backs can't diagnose the actual pain claimed by their owners. Personally, I have horrible-looking MRI studies of my knees and almost no pain and no need for medication. However, all of this is irrelevant. Physically disabled or not, she is clearly *mentally* and *socially* disabled and that is what makes her undeniably unemployable. Can you imagine Mrs. Black Knife working in a clerical pool or any other communal work setting?"

Both the judge and social worker nodded in agreement. They were more than happy to agree with my testimony if it got them off this case and out of Mrs. Black Knife's line of fire. I had given them a graceful exit; everything I had just said was plausible and defendable to whatever powers they had to answer to, especially after the Mrs.'s performance.

The judge made no effort to cover his eagerness to leave this case by banging his gavel, and declaring "Disability granted." Whereupon, both he and the social worker bee-lined it straight for the exit.

Chapter 12: On the Road with Mrs. Black Knife

Joel's stark writings opened a window into a world that I would have otherwise never known. I grew to admire him as much as I liked him. He was only about thirty and so morbidly obese that he literally needed to stuff himself into the passenger seat of my car with the seat set back as far as it would go. He didn't drive—he could never have fit behind a steering wheel—and that gave me opportunities for some quality time by offering to take him where he needed to go from time to time. It wasn't long before we became good friends.

About six months after we'd met, the Black Knifes moved to Seattle where Joel's plays were being produced at an avant-garde theater, and where he became the resident dramaturge.

Then, in the summer of 1990, he mentioned that his wife was planning to drive from Seattle to a piece of land they owned near Flathead Lake in Montana. It was a great opportunity for me to tie in a visit to see him and then catch a ride with Mrs. Black Knife out to the dinosaur camp where Madelaine had been volunteering all summer. The only way I would get to see Madelaine that summer was if I went to her, and therefore it was kismet that the Black Knifes agreed to take me if I helped with the driving. The plan was that the Mrs. would detour and drop me at Jack Horner's dig site for four to five days. Madelaine got Dr. Horner's permission to have me stay there at the encampment and I was excited. When I landed in Seattle, the Mrs. picked me up at the airport in the van we would be travelling in and took me back to her and Joel's apartment.

    I was not expecting the scene I walked into. Their apartment—a little one-bedroom deal on the first floor—was in a decent part of town. But what bowled me over when I walked through the front door was that not a single item of clothing or kitchenware was stored in a closet or cupboard. Everything was everywhere, strewn on tables, sofas, or the floor. It made walking through the apartment a matter of gingerly tiptoeing on, over, or around clothes, pots and pans, papers, whatever. It wasn't even that it was dirty, just general mass confusion.

    I ended up spending that night in a motel, because to say there was no space for me to sleep in their apartment would be an understatement. However, the next day, Mrs. Black Knife was up early to pack for our trip to Montana and the plan was to launch at noon.

Six months before, the Mrs. had been diagnosed with breast cancer. She handled it like she handled all threats: with defiance. It became her mission to beat it and she went about searching ferociously for the exact right alternative medicine that would prove all those allopathic medical bastards wrong. It was just my fate to land right smack in the middle of her war zone precisely when she needed her enemy embodied. She proceeded to overwhelm me with an endlessly expanding litany of desperate, hair-brained treatments.

She had turned the van into a moveable apothecary, loaded with every conceivable would-be medicine, including gallons of pure water and a smudge pot. Her mattress took up most of the space south of the front seats. And her packing, under the circumstances of total apartment chaos, took until early evening to complete. We might never have left if I hadn't found her injured smudge pot buried under a pile of papers on a desk.

All this time, Joel remained tucked neatly in the background, just out of chaos' reach. I saw very little of him, which I regretted because I had looked forward to hearing about his new work. My prime motivation had been to visit Madelaine and see Dr. Horner's dinosaur dig, but the trip was beginning to assume a drama all of its own. Something told me that some unexpected theatre was in store along the way. Any illusion of control over my life was snuffed out pretty quickly.

Once on our way, I was treated to an exhibition of virtuoso driving. Water bottle forever in hand, the Mrs. would swig down a gulp or two every thirty seconds (to wash away her cancer)—most often on the hairpin turns as we rose out of Seattle heading east. Eyes thrust skyward, around and around we would go. All this led to high anxiety for me and frequent road stops to water the grass by the Mrs. I began to calculate that at our pace, a two day journey to reach Montana would triple in length.

Finally, what felt like months later, we arrived at the Horner dinosaur dig. Madelaine had arranged to meet the Mrs. and me at a local trading post near the dig, at such-and-such a time on such-and-such a date. All my nagging of Mrs. Black Knife to speed up and stop guzzling water only made her surlier. She drank more, peed more, and took her sweet revengeful time.

Madelaine was royally pissed at our three-hour late arrival as well—though after the trip we'd just had I was thankful to arrive at all. The Volkswagen Beetle I had given her looked totally demolished compared to when I first bought it, although it was never much of a looker to begin with. It made me wonder what she'd gotten up to out here in the wilderness.

The last ten miles to Jack Horner's dig was across private land, over makeshift bridges that spanned wild streams, and across open prairies without roads. As the Mrs. & I followed the blue bug through the backcountry, it seemed a wonder that it still had wheels. Madelaine flew over the irregular terra firma, rocks, board bridges, streambeds, etc. I pondered how anyone could track their way across the unmarked terrain. Finally, at dusk, we arrived at camp.

Once there, I very much anticipated the parting of ways with Mrs. Black Knife. She, however, immediately glommed onto Madelaine and the other dinosaur groupies after realizing that they had awakened her up-to-now dormant passion to be an archeologist. She was not leaving, come hell or high water. A huge brouhaha ensued, between the Mrs. and the rest of the camp, one that I flatly refrained from engaging in. In the end, the rules regarding intruders were bent, and the Mrs. was allowed to stay one night. Madelaine and the other Horners blamed me for introducing this tree trunk of human trouble into their midst.

Later that evening, Mrs. Black Knife, Madelaine, and I went to a cookout at another dinosaur encampment. While there, the Mrs. asked me to come into the woods for a tête-à-tête. All I could expect was a verbal or physical beating and so I declined the offer. A few hours later, on the way back to our camp, Madelaine and the Mrs. had it out. I can't remember any of the issues or how the fight began, but it was a dilly. I hid in the back seat. The next day, the Mrs. left. She scorned me by not saying goodbye, while she and Madelaine buddied it up until she whirled out.

Madelaine in nature impressed me as much as she had at the cottage in Pease. She had a little tent off to herself. She cooked for the Horner community and went about the digging expeditions. She towed me along and taught me the rudiments of finding and unearthing dinosaur bones. I "worked" a fertile field and found two or three bones of minor rate. Madelaine was my mentor and I loved it and her. That night, we made love—it couldn't be called just sex—for the first time and the last.

I noticed earlier that evening that one of the cowboys in the camp was looking at Madelaine forlornly from a distance. I can only assume he was her summer partner, put temporarily on hold while her "steady" boyfriend came to visit.

A few days later, Madelaine drove me in the blue bug to the local airport to catch a four-seater plane to a bigger airport so I could journey on to Minneapolis. Later that summer, both Madelaine and the bug eventually made it back to town together.

Chapter 13: Madelaine Returns

In the spring of 1990, before she went on her dinosaur dig, Madelaine had taken me aside. "Dick needs a place to live," she asked, "can you take him in? No one's living in your basement. He drinks, but he's not a problem."

Dick worked for Image Premastering Service (IPS), the company Madelaine had introduced me to, where years later I would let The Voice take over during a board meeting—leading to the cops showing up. Dick was somewhere near thirty years of age, a second-degree relative of Edward Sheriff Curtis, the famous photographer of American Indian life. Dick, too, had photographed American Indians and lived with them in the state of Wisconsin. Dick's eye had both the training and genetics that well-served IPS's needs, where they stored high quality museum images in analog format on CDs.

Dick had a girlfriend that Madelaine had fixed him up with, but women and sex were not his thing—photography and booze were. When he got loaded he disappeared into my basement apartment—no noise, no distraction. What did he do drunk behind those closed doors?

"Meet me at Tracy's, Dr. Z. We can have dinner and a drink or two," Dick requested of me one day. Tracy's, Dick's watering hole, was a "locals" bar and grill, with pinball machines, a pool table, chicken and hamburger baskets with fries, and grungy toilets. East Franklin Ave in Minneapolis was a lower class but mixed neighborhood that included aging hippies and a large food co-operative, the Seward Community Co-op. For me, dinner ala Tracy's meant a medium rare hamburger along with a pile of fries in a filigreed red plastic basket lined with grease repelling restaurant paper. I smothered the fries with salt and pepper-laced ketchup and dipped the burger in its own mound of ketchup. The whole disaster got washed down with Cuba Libre—rum, coke, and lime. Heaven on Earth!

"Dr. Z, can I borrow your canoe?" Dick asked me as soon as we had started eating. "I got a job taking photographs of a stretch of the Wolf River in Wisconsin that runs through an Indian Reservation. The Indians want to block a mining operation they say will pollute the river. The photos are to support the case that the river should be kept pristine, be designated a natural scenic river."

"Sure, Dick, I don't use the canoe much anymore," I answered. "It's left over from the days my ex-wife and I would spend the first week in June each year portaging in the Boundary Waters. *Me fish; woman clean and cook.* I'm pretty sure that those vacations were where the roots of my marital failure took hold."

At summer's end, Madelaine returned from dinosaur camp homeless. Her volunteer job had left her broke, unable to pay her rent. As usual, she put her recurring dilemmas on my doorstep—quite literally, this time. "I want to move into your basement apartment. Tell Dick he has to move. I'll help him find another space," Madelaine flatly stated. *Betrayal* was my first thought about throwing Dick out. Rapidly following was, *Oh, no. Madelaine in the basement of my sanctuary—where would I hide from her then? She'll be all over me.* Saying "no" to Madelaine was reflex, yet I hesitated. Madelaine was my spark plug. My sexual and intellectual workout partner. She fed me offbeat venture deals and introduced me to the intellectual in-crowd. Being Madelaine's man turned the heads of lots of machers, lots of movers and shakers. I often felt like Proust's Charles Swann with his courtesan Odette. To quote Stu Goldman, a very wealthy and well thought of member of the Jewish business and philanthropic communities of Minneapolis: "You're dating Madelaine! She's a fine woman, good for you." And for good measure, he gave me a twinkle of his left eye. Did Stu *schtup* Madelaine? Did he have her dance for him in her youth, dressed only in her underpants? Did she give him as good blow jobs as she gave me? That seemed to be the innuendo in his sincerely congratulatory remarks.

Though maybe the innuendo was mine, adding fuel to my erotic fantasies about Madelaine. Would denying Madelaine refuge in my basement mean no more Madelaine? I sensed her demand was an all or nothing deal. Tortured, I still knew that my gut screamed, *no*. Eventually my larynx caught up with my intuition.

Madelaine quickly found another roost that provided her a setting more suited to her needs. She could live rent free with Evangeline Adler, a resourceful, eclectic art administrator who had recently bought a commercial building called the Balto. Located in South

Minneapolis, she got the building for next to nothing as part of some urban renewal project. She and Madelaine knew each other prior to Madelaine moving in and were similar enough in spirit to be great friends. Both had been married and had one child. Both were since divorced, Madelaine from a wife-beater, she claimed. Evangeline spoke of her marriage as "based on lust" and I gathered it ended, in her mind, when the lust did.

I sensed that Madelaine moving into Balto meant she'd move away from me and eventually be lost. Over the next six months, my prophecy played itself out. Still, in the back of my primordial, intuitive mind, what was rumbling to the surface was frightening but necessary—almost ordained.

At Balto, Evangeline established a home, a haven for the intelligentsia of the artsy community. There were parties, hangouts, marijuana, gays and lesbians—the fringe world, infused with a sexuality that called to me like a siren. It also scared my down-to-earth, restrained, scientifically-trained psyche. I watched as Madelaine was absorbed by Balto's "risqué" social world while leaving me, an outsider who occupied a mundane, socially isolated, sexually repressed world, behind.

And of course, there was a man. Nick. Evangeline had hired him to help her rehabilitate Balto. To Evangeline and Madelaine, he was a brilliant, disturbed, sexually-blessed handyman, whom Evangeline supposedly had for a lover in the past. To me, he was the embodiment of evil, of primal sexual lust!

Madelaine was turning forty at the time she moved into the Balto and was still a "piece of ass." She maintained her tense muscular body by exercising furiously for several hours a day. Her squinty, flashing eyes and large, expressive mouth were full of allure.

Of course, Nick and Madelaine became fast friends. It was clear that they were intrigued with each other, that they shared much, ever learning from one another. Nick spent many nights at the Balto, smoking marijuana with Madelaine and sleeping over. After her move, Madelaine spoke so excitingly about him that, rather than her current lover, I felt like a confidante listening to stories about her new lover. Each new adventure stabbed at me. "Nick has this wonderfully ingenious invention that he uses to run his business. Nick is a wizard at backgammon, but I finally figured out how to outwit him. Nick has slept with tons of women; they can't resist him." Why did she tell me these things? To hurt me? To make me jealous? I could only assume she was sexually involved with Nick and this drove me to vivid sexual fantasies. Madelaine never admitted to sleeping with him even though I told her that if she wanted to it was her business and I would drop out. What else could I do?

Still, Madelaine shocked me about a month after moving into the Balto when she told me in a very matter-of-fact, out-of-the-blue manner, "I don't want to have sex with you for now, though we might renew the sexual part of our relationship in the future." No more was said; she gave no reason. I didn't feel I had the right to demand one of her. Truthfully, our sexual relations were never very satisfying, except for our first encounters and that one episode in Montana. I always felt that to Madelaine our sexual encounters were something akin to performance art. Did she have real organisms? She seemed detached, always observing, scheming. She knew what a man wanted and made sure they got it. Still, her sudden denial of our sexual relationship jolted me, making me fantasize that she was having sexual relations with others.

I was not mad at her; I knew I didn't want to live with her. But a mild depression came over me, nothing like what I sensed when my relationship with Kathy, my first wife, crashed. Having experienced my first and worst depression when Kathy left, I predicted that this downer would be less horrendous, shorter. After all, didn't Madelaine and I have a much less intense involvement? And there were no children, though we had dated for four years.

About four weeks into the mild depression, I received a call from my 20-year-old daughter, Gabrielle, who was in her fourth year in theatre school at NYU. She had been lucky enough to win the last opening to spend six months of her senior college year studying in Paris. We hadn't had many opportunities to speak openly with each other since she had moved out to go to college. I felt a need to open my heart to her. "I have always loved you and always will," I said. I cried a bit with this revelation and I think she did too. By the time I hung up, my depression, like a veil over my emotions, miraculously lifted.

About ten years later, my former tenant, Dick, brought my canoe back to Minneapolis, tied to the top of his rusty van. The canoe looked no worse for wear all those years. I had no place to store it. "Nice of you to try and return the canoe, but you keep it," I told him. That's the last I saw of Dick or the canoe—so far.

Chapter 14: Africa

Madelaine was now past tense to me, even though we remained wary friends. As I went through the withdrawal of having her as an everyday presence in my life, I felt the scales rebalance themselves. My anxiety grew less every day and I filled my time with new things, including stepping back out into the world of dating women again. By the time my friend, Max, invited me to join him at a local African nightclub, I was ready.

Over the loud sounds of African music, Max yelled, "Steve!" as he grabbed my elbow and pulled me across the room toward a stunning black woman. "Steve, meet Theodora, my sexy young friend from Tanzania."

My heart stuttered a little as I smiled at her and shook her hand. She was moving to the beat of the song in a red dress that was so low in the back I could see the sweet swell of her buttocks. My own body immediately responded. I was glad it was dark in the club. How the hell a geek like Max knew this beauty was a mystery, but my admiration for him went up a notch.

"Every Wednesday night, they play strictly African music so we Africans have a place to hang out in Minneapolis," he had explained previously. Max was a native of Lusaka, Zambia, and worked as a research veterinarian at Protatek, a start-up company making vaccines for animal diseases similar to malaria. It's where we met and became friends.

Protatek was the brainchild of a man named Bill Smith, who I had nicknamed *The Minneapolis Clown Prince of Business*. Smith had made his money early in life through inheritance and working in the financial sector. Once he considered himself "rich enough," he gave up stodgy bankers and made the glamorous world of venture capital funding his playground.

Smith was an imposing man: 6'3" in height and not quite corpulent. With his underlying football player's physique, he was able to wear his obesity well. He was brilliant, outgoing, and liked by most. He had a way of making you feel that he saw something unique and special in you that no one else could see. I shared an office suite in Minnetonka with him and three other businessmen and it wasn't long before we'd sniffed each other out; he had the work habits of a President Emeritus who drifted through the corridors of his former dynasty, looking for someone to distract. He'd meander over to my office with some ersatz piece of news, shoot the bull for a while, plump up my ego the way a housewife would plump couch cushions and then, concluding that his housekeeping chores were done for the day, he'd disappear off to the golf course. On one of those particularly dynastic days, he appointed me to be chairman of a company he had recently created: Protatek.

"You know, Steve, people respect you because you're a doctor," he said out of the blue. "So as chairman of Protatek, you'll run circles around those MBA boys."

Why not? I thought. *What did those MBA guys know about amoebas and vaccines and antibodies?* So, without leaving my desk, without any experience, I gained a new company to run and some new employees to get to know.

That's how I got to know Max. He was the most intriguing of all the researchers in this new company, and it wasn't long before I found out he was single and always cruising for booty. I couldn't have asked for a better prowling partner. He was an instinctive flirt, raised in a culture where men chased skirts as a hobby, and I admired the effortlessness with which he related to women.

Even though I was pushing fifty, women had always been inscrutable and mysterious. The only two women I grew up knowing well were my mother and my sister and they were hardly sources of sexual education. From high school through college and medical school, I'd only attended all male schools—Stuyvesant High School, Union College, and lastly, SUNY's Downstate Medical School with its 150 nerdy men and three nerdy women in the class of 1966. I had married my wife just out of medical school. Frankly, I'd always assumed that most women didn't like sex, unless they were *shikzas*, gentile women. Most of my short forays into sexual ecstasy in my teens and early twenties were initiated by the opposite sex, so I had little experience in corrupting women. I had no idea how to decipher their needs and not a clue how to beguile them into bed. As far as I was concerned, they were the unfathomable gatekeepers of all that was luscious and off-limits. So, Max, the Zambian Casanova, was a welcome mentor.

Which is how I found myself opposite this jewel named Theodora. Before she even turned and smiled at me, I was hopelessly perpendicular and stiff. The only thoughts in my mind were of nuzzling her soft curves and tasting the salt on her skin. With supreme effort, I controlled myself and managed to say, "Hello."

"Hi, Stephen. You like to dance?" she asked, her sinuous body undulating to a rhythm that seemed to have been born inside of her.

"Ah, not now," I managed and then I offered to buy her a drink. We stood at the bar, me aware that I was sweating in all of the wrong places, and her with soft dew on her face while she rocked with the beat of the *djembe*. She seemed very confident and at ease. I asked her what she "did," as everyone did in the '80s when yuppie-ism was at its zenith.

"I'm looking for work right now," she said and then her face lit up as she added, "Maxwell told me you could help me get a job."

Well, a woman who gets right to the point, I thought.

"Oh, really? I'd love to hear about you and what you're looking for. But...." I leaned in closer to her ear so she could hear me. "This place is too noisy to talk. How about lunch this Friday at the American Café?"

The prowl with Max had been successful.

I knew that Theodora was twenty-three and, being close to fifty myself, I was quite certain that nothing was going to happen. But I still looked forward to sitting across from her and drooling in my mind. I told myself to keep it to business.

The American Café was located at the crossroads of two major highways where traffic going into downtown Minneapolis snarled every rush hour, so it was the perfect place for the power breakfast. Located six miles west of Minneapolis was the wealthiest of Minnesota's 10,000 lakes, Lake Minnetonka. Its cadre of CEOs, CFOs, COOs, consultants, et al., jammed the American Café from 7 a.m. to 9:30 a.m. every morning to avoid the traffic leading to downtown. Schmoozing was the *potins de'jour*—as rumor-filled business palaver spread from table to table like honeybees spread pollen across a field.

Theodora was prompt—11:45 a.m.—on the nose. We sat across the table from each other with the paltry intimacy of a booth. She wore a more modest dress than the one she'd worn the night before, which was appropriate but privately disappointing. She was surprisingly petite—only around 5'2", something I had not noticed the night before—but her beauty and poise gave her the presence of a much taller person.

I asked her what she would like for lunch as I scanned the menu.

"Coffee will do," she said, signaling that she was here for business.

"You need a job, you said. What's your work background?

"I really haven't worked very much. I spent eight years in London in boarding school and college."

"Really? That must have been quite an adjustment. I mean going from Africa to London."

"Yes and no. I was prepared for it as two of my brothers had gone to the same school before me. But I have always wanted to come to the U.S., so when I graduated a college friend of mine invited me to come stay."

I asked her a few general questions to get a grasp of her experience and any skills I could use to tout her as a good risk, and then said, "I know a *few* people who might be able to hire you since you obviously have no problem with English but, I have to warn you—this is the Midwest. Being black here is not what you would call an asset. However, being from Africa may be appealing. I'll make some calls and see if we get lucky."

She smiled and said, "That is very kind of you." She glanced off into some faraway place for a moment and then focused back on me as she continued, "There is something else I would like to talk to you about." I could immediately feel the conversation shift and become more personal by her body language.

"In London, I had a relationship with a fellow my age, a schoolmate. Now, I want a relationship with an older man who can teach me new things." She smiled almost shyly at me and added, "I am willing to try most anything."

I let that thought settle in my rattled brain. Here was a new breed of woman, one who was in charge of her own sexuality. Of all the men in constant pursuit of her, Theo had chosen *me*. My self-esteem soared.

But all I could manage was, "We'll see about that."

A week later, with Theo's proposal disrupting all my efforts to concentrate on my work, I finally called her and asked her out on a date. At first, she hesitated, so I said, "Look, there's no obligation. We can enjoy each other's company to whatever level you feel comfortable."

That closed the deal. She agreed.

Who are you Theo? I thought to myself as I slid her chair under her at the restaurant. She was wearing another dress that was well above her knees with a scooped back that was well *below* the small of her back.

Theo wanted to talk. Her face came to life as she told me about her twenty-three years on Earth. In her colorfully accented English, exotic words tumbled out of her mouth—*chieftain, Chagga tribe, witchdoctor, jungle fever, malaria, hippopotamus, black mamba,* ancestral lands called *kihamba*, *Ruwa*, the name for both their god and the sun, *Tanzania,* her country. Visions of black flesh, painted Bantu warriors danced to the dum-dum-dum-dum-dum-dum beat of drums while ancestral eyes glared up from the underworld. She talked about living in the shadow of *Killy*—the local nickname for Mount Kilimanjaro—and tales about the many and diverse travelers from every corner of the world who would visit to climb this behemoth.

Then, she made her titillating confession.

"It was not *one* fellow student I slept with, but many. Men of all ilks," she admitted.

I wanted to be the next one.

"Will you come home with me, Theo?"

She hesitated. I wondered why. *Hadn't she led me to her mysteries? Would she now deny me entrance? Was she being coy? Or was this her style of foreplay?*

Please say yes, I prayed silently—and she did.

When my wife left a decade before, she left everything behind: the kids, the house, the furniture, knickknacks, *everything*. My children had grown up and left too. Now it was just me in my suburban rambler. I rented part of the house with kitchen privileges to Dick, but that evening the house was dark when Theo and I arrived.

Theo headed directly toward the kitchen, hopped up, and perched on the counter with her legs open and her underpants exposed. My knees were threatening to buckle, but I had the presence of mind to remember that while this might be a dream come true, it could turn into my worst nightmare if I ignored the fact that Theo was a sexually active woman from Africa. Precautions had to be taken.

I was so infatuated with Theo that I told her I would give her one of the large amber beads I collected for each time we were together. I said, "Once you have my entire collection, it will be time for both of us to move on. No hanging on. No false promises. But you'll have the beads to remind you of this time together with me."

My fatalism surprised me and yet it also delighted. I knew that Theo and I had to seize the moment. Intuitively, I knew that past a certain point, our lust for each other would begin to fade. The key was not to make more of our relationship than what it was—lust for lust's sake.

After that first night with Theo, she told me she was low on cash and asked me to loan her $200. She promised she'd repay me when she got a job.

Was I scammed? Sex for cash? Was I a fool to think Theo slept with me because she *liked* me? An easy mark she knew she could manipulate? Was I *that* simple, *that* egotistical, that I didn't see the quid pro quo coming?

Theo could have chosen a laundry list of men, men who would have been glad to support her, but she chose me. I quickly got over my bruised ego, but the thrill of conquest had been badly deflated. *I'll help you Theo*, I thought to myself, *but as an uncle, not a lover.*

I tried to find Theo a job with my friend and fellow HDII board member, Harold, who ran an early-stage biotech company. But he was blunt about why he couldn't give her a job:

"I could not have Theo around. I'd always be trying to screw her."

She eventually *did* land a job at a bank and afterwards, we spent one more night together. Three months later, Max told me she had returned to Africa. A year after that, while I was in Europe, she left a message that she was back in Minneapolis for a visit and wanted to see me. Our arcs never crossed again after that.

Before I die, I'd love to visit her in Chagga country, at the foot of Kilimanjaro so we could hold hands and look into each other's eyes one last time.

Chapter 15: Attack of the Dybbuk

A few weeks after we broke up, in the fall of 1990, Madelaine and I decided to have dinner together. For me it was a chance to find out if there was any hope of getting back to our old stand-still, absurd as that was. What was in it for Madelaine? A free meal out? The night before, I had what I characterized as a premonition. I envisioned that Madelaine would be provoked to uncontrollable rage at me and that a hidden beast in her would expose itself and attack me on the right side of my head, at which point I could inflict injury upon it. In so doing, I would help Madelaine free herself from its grip. My image of the beast's attack was startlingly clear, but it did not feel prophetic. I rationalized that it was an expression of my belief that Madelaine was trapped by some of the horrors of her upbringing. It was months later that The Voice made itself known for the first time.

I suspected the cause of Madelaine's rage would be Theo. Madelaine had come to know of Theo about a week before my premonition. Weeks before—right after Madelaine said that she wanted to stop having sex with me—she also said that she'd been unfaithful only once. Recently, she had slept with an acquaintance of hers, a farmer friend from the Dakotas. I pondered "the why" of her admission and settled on the thought that Madelaine wanted to be bluntly open and honest, a virtue of sorts. In my mind, I applauded her honesty and felt I needed to reciprocate.

The next time we were together, I told her about Theo. Her initial response was something like, "Oh, how exciting." Then I overheard her whisper to herself: "I need to process this."

Regardless of our past, I felt I loved Madelaine and wanted her to fulfill her "mind's potential." It seemed I enjoyed associating with characters whose brilliant potential was thwarted by what I saw as an emotional disability, a Shakespearian tragic flaw, and the thought that somehow I could rescue them.

During my emotional upheaval, brought on by the ending of Madelaine's and my relationship, I spilled out my heart to my bilingual (English and Yiddish) speaking mother who, up to that time, knew nothing of

Madelaine. She was shocked by my portrayal. She didn't mince words: she was convinced that Madelaine was a *dybbuk*—Yiddish for devil—or at the very least, possessed by one.

On the night of our dinner, Madelaine and I chose to eat at the new Market BBQ. The old Market BBQ had been an institution in downtown Minneapolis since 1954. Its prize-winning pork ribs, its large collection of porcine dolls and statues, its attached striptease hall, its seedy downtown location, all gave it landmark status. It had since moved—original furniture and all—one mile south to Nicollet Avenue on the outskirts of downtown, to make way for a basketball arena and parking complex. Minneapolis was trying to clean up its core and the Market had to move on.

When I stepped into the new restaurant I noticed that it had still retained its cozy, low-class flavor. Dim yellow lighting, its wooden tables and booths worn ragged by years of use, checkerboard oilcloths on the tables, piggy dolls tucked here and there. An ancient but very well preserved rococo juke box, full of oldies, was actuated by old-fashioned flip page consoles at each booth. The restaurant had lots of square feet per booth and table, lots of open, quiet space and down-home weary waitresses to fit the atmosphere. The ribs were served on flat, dark-brown colored plastic serving trays lined with animal grease resistant oilpaper. Ribs, French fries, coleslaw, ketchup, hot and medium BBQ sauce in plastic squeeze bottles, toothpicks and individually packaged alcohol wipes, all found a spot for themselves on the paper liner—no dishes necessary. The Market's signature crisp BBQ pork ribs, exuding the odor of burnt pig flesh and made from the family's secret formula, provoked an eating frenzy, a complete abandonment of etiquette!

At dinner that evening, Madelaine and I sat across from each other at a small table for two. She seemed her usual talkative, upbeat, manic self. "What'll it be, a half or a whole slab?" challenged our waitress.

"I'll take a full dose, what about you?" I asked Madelaine.

"The same. I could eat a bear." She ate her rib dinner with a carnivore-like fervor—teeth exposed, head almost in her tray. Suddenly, without provocation, Madelaine stopped eating and began to sputter on, louder and louder: "You motherfucker, whoring around with that Chagga, bitch. I hate your guts. I'll cut your balls off." Her facial expression became more and more contorted as she simultaneously leaned threateningly over the table, her head thrust forward, mouth open, her eyes narrow slits, staring directly at me. I felt like her prey, as though I had replaced her ravenous desire for her pork ribs. My mind reeled. I tried to conjure up a way to immediately escape from her presence. I was about to be bitten or worse.

Then, in mid-sentence and mid-striking posture, Madelaine froze. A perplexed look came over her and after a long pause she retreated from her suspended state and collapsed back into her chair. Then, with a blank stare on her face, she began to vomit out, at an unbelievable velocity, what sounded to be verbal garbage. I could barely understand a word. The spell lasted some thirty seconds. What content I could grasp was related to predictions by Nostradamus, whose name was mentioned several times.

At the end of Madelaine's verbal explosion, she sat dumbstruck in her chair. She then had four or five spasms that traversed through her whole body. Following these, she was able to converse in slow motion, requesting that we go. Little else was said. Still startled by Madelaine's bizarre behavior, I had no idea what to expect. Perhaps a repeat performance was about to occur. I drove her home, fearful all the way. But I didn't need to worry; on arriving at the Balto building, she said a short goodbye and disappeared.

It was hard not to see Madelaine's violent attack as her "devil" getting loose. Certainly I was being targeted. A good part of her violence toward me was verbal and I am deaf in my left ear. Therefore, her attack was heard by my right "good" ear. Would it be stretching a point to say that her devil, her *dybbuk*, had been provoked and exposed itself, and, in mid-attack, been struck down and forced to vomit up a litany of verbal garbage? Would Madelaine be better off for this "exorcism?"

Or perhaps this was carrying things metaphorically too far. At a time in the past, I remember that Madelaine had told me, and some others as well, that there was another person in her that rarely had been seen by anyone. I never knew how she exactly characterized this other person, but it seemed she had a need to hide this other, or, at least be wary of it. Whether it was the devil or something else, *dybbuk* seems as good a characterization as any.

Chapter 16: Six Psychic Sessions To Love

About three or four days after the Market BBQ incident, Madelaine called me—something she hadn't done for months. She invited me out to lunch during her noon break at the graphics company where she was working. I jumped at the opportunity.

Madelaine wore dark sunglasses to lunch—unusual fall attire especially as it was a cloudy day. Maybe she felt they would prevent me from looking into her eyes and causing another "seizure." To my surprise, Madelaine was warm and friendly, something I didn't expect after our explosive scene at the Market BBQ.

But then, in the midst of lunch, she switched gears on me.

"If you ever tell anyone about what happened at dinner, I'll kill you."

I was taken aback, feeling threatened and wary. Madelaine possessed a gun and knew how to use it. But I also had my curiosity piqued. Why did Madelaine so desperately want to keep that moment a secret? Sensing that it would be better to stay quiet, I didn't answer her threat one way or the other. She then did a 180 by saying, "You're the most open-minded man I have ever known." With this extraordinary compliment from Madelaine, my curiosity index went off the chart.

After lunch, she invited me to her work place, a large office room divided into cubicles. She gave me a tour of her cubicle with its collection of pictures of friends—me included—and her new computer. She then took me to meet the denizens of other cubicles, her co-workers. Each time, she introduced me as if I was her prize, her boyfriend. Though I played along, smiling and chatting, I was actually overcome by Madelaine's turnabout. She had never shown such feelings toward me. Her affection made no sense, as I had just distanced myself from her emotional sphere. Now I began to wonder if she truly did love me, or want me to be her lover again. Should I seek her out? Throw caution to the wind and restart our affair?

It was now late fall of 1990. My fiftieth birthday loomed ahead of me. Some eight years before, I had predicted that this date would mark the beginning of a sea of changes in my life. It was déjà vu, as I had made the same prediction regarding reaching age forty, when my first marriage ended and everything went to hell in a hand basket.

My life as a venture capitalist was getting difficult, unexciting, actually boring and not all that successful. I had no energy to raise another venture fund and was, I felt, an outsider to the staid venture capital money managers in Minnesota. For one, I was an MD and most of them were MBAs. We didn't speak the same language. More so, my nature was that of a maverick. I thought highly of myself, believing that I knew better and I relied more on my intuition than calculated assessments to pick winning venture investments. Thus, I had no one else to rely on, and no new projects to look forward to; all my present venture capital funds were fully invested.

What I wanted to do at this juncture in my life was to become an emotionally sensitive individual who could transform himself into an artist as I had dreamed of becoming in the past. I believed I had it in me to become an inspired, unique writer. Did I have the driving force, the sensitivity to create? How did artists sustain their emotional and financial being without the achievements that filled my world? But when I looked at my heroes, they weren't J.P. Morgan, but were instead visionaries such as W. Averell Harriman, Albert Schweitzer, and most certainly artists such as Gauguin and Joseph Conrad.

I remembered a photography contest held at Mt. Zion hospital in San Francisco when I was an internal medicine resident in 1969. I entered a beautifully arranged black and white photo of lily pads. Joe, my intern, entered a picture of his daughter running across a field. Her image was blurred, full of motion, full of passion. He won the award, hands down. I felt insensitive, ashamed of myself.

Planning and executing change in an orderly manner was not my style. I ran until I couldn't, then when everything fell apart—which was what was in the process of happening to me—I changed, because I had to.

Seeing Madelaine had stirred me once again. I called her up after seeing her at her office, and we met the next week. No sex, but that was okay. The problem was the setting at the Balto building, her present abode. Through our entire visit, Nick was lurking about, clearly agitated by Madelaine's attention to me. He apparently spent a good deal of his time at the Balto and a good deal of that time with Madelaine. While he was in another room, she again detailed her growing relationship with him. She again told me of his sexual escapades with countless women, never, however, admitting to having sex with him herself. She asked my advice on how to deal with his violent, confrontational outbursts. I told her, "Look him straight in the eyes and tell him to stick it up his rear. Stare him down. He's a coward and will retreat."

It worked, as far as I know. For me, all the encounter did was make me both a voyeur and an active participant to their seemingly intoxicating relationship. Thinking of them made me depressed and severely anxious. I sensed that Madelaine enjoyed tormenting me with Nick. I envisioned her and him having extraordinary S&M-style sex. After all, he was the violent sort and she was physically very strong.

When I asked one of Madelaine's confidants why she bothered with me, I was informed she did so for a free meal. The revelation stung. I knew I should walk away, but I couldn't; I had already freed myself from Madelaine once, and now I felt myself getting sucked back into her web, helpless to leave again. I was a wreck. After a few more Nick-filled encounters at the Balto, I concluded I truly loved Madelaine, but she no longer could be mine. Maybe she never even really loved me. Much worse yet, she was entranced with that bastard, Nick, and I was having my emotions rubbed into their sordid, Balto-based, den of inequity affair.

When I was alone with my thoughts, I tried to vilify her. Madelaine is a whore, a courtesan, selfish, unable to love, manipulative, cold, unfeeling, a lousy mother! Downright evil. Again and again I rummaged through my four years of knowing her, looking for defaming labels. None truly stuck. Worse, to my horror, those same labels seemed to stick to me. Was Madelaine my female equal? Was she my soul's mirror?

I finally decided I could not go on in my present state of anxiety. I could withdraw from any and all contact with Madelaine or I could go to Madelaine and let her know my feelings. I decided I had to tell her I loved her, the second woman in my life that I had ever loved. Kathy, my ex-wife, was the first, aside from my mother who I had, for a while, hated for the joy she took in beating me at pinochle, a card game she taught me to play.

In a state of severe agitation, I asked Madelaine to go with me to a neighborhood German beer house, called The Black Forest. It was evening and the restaurant was noisy and crowded. We sat in the darkened bar area at a small, elevated, round table meant only for drinking. Immediately, I poured my heart out to an unprepared Madelaine. I told her I loved her, that she was only the second woman I had ever loved and, "You don't have to love me back if you can't, I just want to clear my heart." I cried freely through it all.

She was stunned, silent. I felt relieved and in a bit of a trance. At that moment the waitress showed up to inform us that our table for dinner was ready, providing a timeout for both Madelaine and I to reload our emotions. When we sat down for dinner, it was clear that it was now Madelaine's turn. She spoke of her life, her upbringing, and I listened attentively. Somewhere during the evening, without a word of such being said, we came to a decision: we would meet regularly to continue digging into Madelaine's past, her childhood, and early adulthood, before I knew her. At one point, I remember feeling like a moth drawn to light. Madelaine shed a tear—the first I had ever seen from her. Not only could I not resist the illumination, but I now had purpose and direction. Apparently, Madelaine felt the same way. That night she kissed me with warm lips.

Our "dance" rules were set. We met weekly at the Balto to continue Madelaine's revelations about her past. Her small, curtained-off bedroom with its dim lighting gave our sessions the feeling of a private séance. That first night, Madelaine told me of the horrors and degradations she had suffered during her childhood. I vowed never to disclose what she said, and even if I had not made such a vow I would not, under any duress, reveal her tormented past. Such was the intimacy of her story.

That first night's conversation made my head swim. It was as though I had entered into the mysterious and convoluted world of Madelaine's mind. I felt as though I was on a magical flying carpet traveling headlong down a very narrow and deep river gorge, barely avoiding collisions at every turn. At last the river flowed through a lush, tranquil valley, the heart of Madelaine's soul, the headwaters of her innocent youth. That night I loved Madelaine with a passion I had never known.

We continued to meet for six weeks. After the sixth session, I realized this would be our last. I expressed to Madelaine that I had done all I could and that the rest was up to her. "People can change," she said. *Not really*, I thought.

But I only stared into Madelaine's eyes and said, "Only time will tell. Time is truth." And I meant it.

Chapter 17: The Computer Schism

Before Madelaine went on her dinosaur dig in the summer of 1990, she had cajoled me into buying her a computer, along with a scanner and printer. At the time personal computers were relatively new, large, and very expensive. The cost of the purchase, $10,000, was discounted because I bought the computer through UMN where I was on the clinical faculty. Madelaine wanted the most and the best, and I acquiesced.

But I didn't do it for free. "I will buy it for you, Madelaine," I told her, "if you promise to do what I need done for my venture fund. Things like quarterly reports, special announcements, not much. Otherwise, it's yours."

She agreed. *"Buy this, buy that, buy this!"* had become her mantra.

Was I a naive nut? I knew Madelaine was a flake and didn't care much about holding down jobs. Deep down, I knew she was using me, but somehow I rationalized the deal could work out. I was also recently flush from a venture killing, which meant loose spending on my part.

That fall and into the winter, Madelaine did a little of the work I required of her. She crafted a fabulous fusion Hanukkah/Christmas greeting card, titled Hanuchris, for the 1990 winter holiday season. My inscription on the cards, optimistic pragmatism: "To a world chuck full of economic 'warfare,' military peace, and planetary love." She also helped me with publishing my venture fund's annual report and fall newsletter.

After the six psychic sessions with Madelaine, I began to sense the supernatural in my daily life. I wrote a love diary to Madelaine that I felt she could sense as I wrote it. When the words and phrases I used were "true," tears would well up in my eyes and wet the written pages. I could feel Madelaine's spirit entering my bedroom and I knew that we were telepathically communicating. Yet just the opposite was occurring in the "real world." After our sessions ended, Madelaine cut me off. She did not call me; she did not answer my calls. She did no further work to pay off the computer I had bought her.

Madelaine's friends, the computer savvy couple, did call me back. "Oh yes, Madelaine has been spending lots of time with us figuring out how to use the computer you bought her," they told me.

"Well, I don't hear from her at all," I said. "She owes me work, damn it!" I felt betrayed: because she didn't finish the work, because those psychic sessions that had meant so much to me seemed so trivial to her.

"Steve, I hate to tell you this," the female half of the couple answered, "but Madelaine never had any intention of working off the cost of the computer. I'm Madelaine's friend, but I don't approve of how she's treating you."

Madelaine's daughter, Laurie, added more salt to my open wounds. "Mom hangs out most evenings at the Balto with Nick working together on your computer." Years later, Madelaine abandoned the computer—it was obsolete by then anyway—and Laurie got possession of it. "Do you want the computer back?" she offered. I thanked her and declined. "It's junk by now, anyway."

But at the time, I was livid, and Laurie's comments delivered the final blow. The thought of Nick and Madelaine bonding over my computer while I was shut out was too much to bear. I was both outraged and paralyzed at the same time. Months passed, and it was early spring. And then, without warning, The Voice suddenly appeared in my life and changed everything.

At one point, The Voice decided to address Madelaine and my problem with her.

"ASK HER OUT TO DINNER," it instructed me. "AT DINNER ASK HER TO MARRY YOU."

"Are you crazy?!" I said aloud. "What if she accepts?! That's the last thing I would want—" But then it occurred to me: that was probably the last thing Madelaine would want too, what with her fear of stirring up her Crohn's Disease.

"YES. DO YOU SEE?" The Voice asked and let a pregnant pause pass.

It suddenly felt like a genius move. By asking her to marry me, I would put the fear of G-d in her. I could get even and finally put an end to our tortured relationship.

The Voice knew its stuff. It had been in my head for a few weeks now, helping me through the board meetings, guiding me toward revelations. So by the time I took Madelaine out to dinner, I trusted it implicitly. I knew it wouldn't steer me wrong.

Madelaine readily accepted my dinner invitation and I went to pick her up at the bad Balto building. Nick, as usual, was lurking about. Upon my arrival, he launched into a frenzied dance, both bizarre and threatening. It must be time for me to get even, I thought. He, too, was apparently distraught over his relationship with Madelaine and hers with me.

Dinner was in a Warehouse District restaurant in downtown Minneapolis. Madelaine and I ordered our food and then clinked our wine glasses.

"To our future," I proclaimed with irony. "I want you to be my wife."

A look of fear and confusion appeared on Madelaine's face. A shudder ran through her body. She suddenly stood up and, without uttering a word, darted out of the restaurant door. It was late April, no more than thirty degrees outside, and Madelaine was two miles from home. She didn't return.

Now I just needed her to cough up my computer.

The next day, I prepared to go over to Madelaine's to retrieve the computer on my own. But when I opened my door, there stood my brother Bobby.

At this point, Dear Reader, we have come full circle. I began this story with my brother at the door, and here he was. Not long after, I was jumping out of his car when he made it clear he wouldn't drive me to Madelaine's. That night the cops were the ones at my door, telling me they were concerned about my health and asking me to come with them.

The Voice was silent. I didn't resist.

Chapter 18: Incarceration

The two St. Louis Park policemen who had come to my house escorted me back to the Hennepin County Psych holding tank—my second visit after what happened at the IPS board meeting. I barely had a chance to settle in when two toughs in white came and got me. "Your brother asked us to take you to the University Hospital," one of them said.

Again, resistance seemed futile and there was no word from The Voice, so I went with them willingly. I was tucked securely into the rear of an ambulance and whisked to the UMN Hospital emergency room, my old stomping grounds—though this time I was definitely on the other side of the fence. The ER clerk asked me for my name, address, and insurance, but The Voice suddenly spoke up just as I was about to answer.

"DO NOT ANSWER ANY OF THEIR QUESTIONS. DO *NOT* LET THEM EXAMINE YOU. DO NOT LET THEM TAKE YOUR BLOOD PRESSURE OR LOOK IN YOUR EYES."

Why not listen? I thought to myself. *I'm just a passenger here. Let's see where The Voice takes me.*

I followed The Voice's instructions and refused to answer the clerk. She tried every which way: nice and sweet, stern and threatening, but I didn't fall for any of it.

It turned out The Voice knew my rights. They could not force me to answer questions or be examined. But I *could* be held there on a 72 hour "visit" ordered by Sid's psychiatrist—the one who'd had a whopping thirty-second snapshot of me, a handshake, and an overdose of Sid's anxiety.

It seemed that having powerful friends was a double-edged sword. In order to lock a person up on a 72-hour hold, someone with medical credibility would have to see clear evidence of the suspect acting in a way that was either a danger to others or a danger to themselves. The rules were pretty strict. But, if you're a physician, especially a physician with a lot of friends and associates in the medical community who are worried about you, they ignore the rules that apply to the regular rabble. I was, I suppose, flattered.

Following my refusals in the University Emergency Room, I was escorted away by two beefy orderlies who'd shown up to replace the cops. I went peacefully, in part because I was outnumbered, but mostly because I was excited to see what was going to happen next. Bookended by my burly lads all the way up to the sixth floor, we perambulated down dingy corridors until we came to a heavily reinforced door that sported an unmarked slot and a buzzer.

A few thwacks on the buzzer and the slot opened. The face on the other side asked for identification. The burlys flashed plastic name cards that hung around their necks, and the door unbolted and swung open. I noticed from the side that it was at least five inches thick—if I were going to escape, it would have to be with the help of a howitzer. I made a mental note to ask someone to smuggle one in.

The boys and I stepped into a florescent-lit corridor that seemed as long as a train and was punctuated with identical closed doors all the way down on both sides. Suddenly, the howitzer door swung shut with a thud that curled the primordial hairs on my balls.

I knew in my gut that on the other side of that locked door was my life up until now. My new life would begin, ominously, here in this psych ward. A shiver sneaked up my spine as a bead of sweat rolled down it.

I wondered why they just didn't bury this place underground; it was so thoroughly inhospitable that it would be more fitting as a jail than a hospital. Nothing on the walls but innocuously colored paint meant to calm the raving lunatic, I supposed. It was hard not to believe that I had, unwittingly, committed some heinous crime. I went over my list of wrongdoings in my head. For certain, I had broken some well-entrenched social conventions—you just don't go around telling people that you're G-d, especially if you're Jewish. But that was hardly a capital crime.

I was led into a narrow room that actually had a window, though it was covered with suicide-proof wire-mesh. There was a bed, a dresser, and a desk. The burly boys confiscated my shoelaces and belt for my own good, and Arlo Guthrie and Sheriff Obie immediately came to mind. I started to hum the tune to "Alice's Restaurant."

Once left alone, I decided it was time for the grand tour. I walked past the nurses' station, the community bathrooms that were unlockable and piss-stained, the "gym," which consisted of one stationary bike, and the dining room. Meals were served three times a day, with one snack in the evening. The grand tour took all of three minutes, so I headed back to my cell.

Before too long, a social worker wearing her "patient advocate" hat, stopped by to explain my rights to me. I knew I was there for a 72-hour hold, but she made it clear that it *could* last twice as long, what with weekends and holidays, and judges' availabilities. Eventually, I would go to a court hearing that would determine whether or not I should be "kept" for a longer period. If I needed to receive neuroleptics, my court hearing would have two parts: one for the incarceration and the other to allow the psychiatrists to force me to take their mind-bending medications. I knew that if I was forced to take neuroleptics I might disappear inside this place and never even realize it.

The Voice was with me constantly as I walked the dingy halls and lay on the narrow bed. It explained that it had caused all the turmoil and troubles for me in order to get me incarcerated. "You really want me in here?" I asked out loud. I couldn't believe what my deaf ear was saying.

"YOU WERE TOO DISTRACTED WITH YOUR FRENETIC BUSINESS DEALS. HERE YOU ARE FREE FROM THOSE DISTRACTIONS, LOCKED UP WHERE YOU CAN'T RUN AWAY. ALL YOUR NEEDS WILL BE TAKEN CARE OF—FOOD, SHELTER, CLOTHES. WE CAN GET ON WITH THE WORK THAT WE NEED TO DO."

How clever this voice was. It had scripted my performance and would continue to do so. It had told me again and again to refuse psychiatric counseling and medications, and to reveal little or nothing about my thoughts to anyone.

When Sid's psychiatrist finally showed up around dinnertime, he explained, patiently, that I was "acting maniacal," that I was speaking too fast with "pressured speech"—a hallmark of manic behavior. My response was to speak exceedingly slow. "I caann taaaalk aaaatt aaany speed I waaaant, and now I want you to put your tail between your legs and get the fuck out of my room."

He sighed and left.

What started as a 72-hour stay at the University slowly became closer to a week. During that time I was fed, clothed, and given free telephone service and mail. I had little to do but finally try and understand what this wild and wonderful voice had in store for me. One thing The Voice made very clear from the get-go was:

"ALL WILL BE TAKEN CARE OF—YOUR STOCK HOLDINGS IN YOUR VENTURE COMPANIES WILL BE PRESERVED, YOUR CHILDREN WILL BE BLESSED. YOUR PARENTS WILL LIVE TO SEE YOU FREED. I WILL, IN TIME, GET YOU OUT OF HERE. NO ONE WILL GET HURT."

When I first heard The Voice I was hesitant and distrustful, wary of the message it was sending me. But by the time I ended up at the University, I'd given myself over to this phenomenon completely. I wanted the Voice in my life. I was a willing passenger to wherever it was taking me!

About five days into my "72-hour" hold I was taken to the Hennepin County Court House—a fiasco from start to finish. Prior to this hearing to determine if I was committable or if I needed forced neuroleptic medication (or both), I received a flurry of uninterruptable memos, letters, pronouncements, and warnings about what was to happen. I signed here and there that I had received the material and understood it.

But I didn't understand any of it. "GET A LAWYER," The Voice said. "ONE WHO DEALS WITH THIS INCARCERATION BS." Sounded like good advice to me. I went about ransacking lawyer listings for ones dealing with incarcerated crazies and found just the man for me at a major Minneapolis law firm. He was the committal king, the one who had handled 100 cases, minimum. He was blunt with me: "Of the cases I have defended, 98% lose in court," he said. "The hearings are rigged. After all, how can a "crazy" breech the testimony of a psychiatrist who gives sworn testimony that you're harmful to yourself or others and that you need to be locked up and drugged!" No mention of fees was brought up, but that was fine; I had bucks in the bank.

The lawyer started by fighting fire with fire. An older psychiatrist was hired to interview me and give his esteemed opinion as a clinical professor of psychiatry at UMN. The shrink spent a dutiful two hours interviewing me. The Voice behaved itself; no mention was made of me being G-d, Jesus, or any other savior. His written evaluation of yours truly boiled down to: "Dr. Zuckerman is no danger to himself or others, there is no need for incarceration, and he may or may not benefit from drug treatment." It couldn't have been stated in a better way—but would it make a difference in court?

The Voice wasn't depending on my lawyer or my consulting shrink. "CALL DR. KAPLAN, YOUR GASTROENTEROLOGIST," it told me, "AND ASK HIM TO SEND OVER THE X-RAYS OF YOUR UPPER GI SERIES THAT SHOWED YOU HAD, IN HIS ESTIMATE, A CANCER OF YOUR TERMINAL JEJUNUM THAT WAS GOING TO KILL YOU AT AGE FORTY!" I wasn't sure what the Voice wanted with them, but I agreed.

The x-rays arrived, the very originals, in a large and very heavy manila folder. At The Voice's instruction, I told the nursing staff that, "these are the x-rays of my head that show a brain tumor." I also bragged to them that I would win at the hearing. "The judge will let me go free," I said. "This is all BS, psychiatry is BS. All they do is to make stupid diagnoses. They should never be allowed to arrest people." I truly believed The Voice would spring me, though I had no idea how.

The trial hearing was preceded by an interview with the court psychiatrist, Dr. Jude. "Your name is familiar," I said. "You used to work with Harley Schear, the neurologist from San Francisco, on over-the-phone

EEG interpretations, didn't you? I was a resident at Mt. Zion Hospital in San Francisco and researched that program." This led to a fifteen minute animated conversation on our crossed paths. Later in the trial I found out Dr. Jude corroborated my University psychiatrist's diagnosis, claiming I was a manic depressive in a manic state.

Some bastard shill, I thought.

The trial did not go well. "Dr. Zuckerman, stop calling the female assistant district attorney and the female medical stenographer, 'sweetheart,'" Judge Grump ordered. Maxwell, my foul-mouthed Zambian friend and business associate, couldn't understand why the assistant district attorney thought my use of foul language was foul, not just English. Madelaine, my girlfriend, the one with the gun, the sexual manipulator, said she became sexually afraid of me. Given a chance at rebuttal, I asked, "Well, why then last summer did you allow me to take you from the rear—not in your rear, in your vagina, doggy style? You weren't at all afraid then?" Silence followed, and a red-faced Madelaine. My brother was my brother. Worried about his idol, his big brother, and wanting to be magnanimous, he still testified in the Zuckerman family style of "pressured speech."

My ex-wife and daughter were witness to the whole trial. I could imagine my ex thinking, *there he goes again, shooting off at the mouth.*

I was getting fed up. *When are you going to tell me what to do so I can win?* I protested to The Voice in my left ear.

"JUST WAIT. I WILL TELL YOU SOON," The Voice calmly reiterated over and over as the trial proceeded to a conclusion. But then all was over and no statement had come from my mentor. Confused, flustered, and discouraged, I was led from the courtroom. At the moment I was led past Judge Grump in his perch, The Voice said, "TELL HIM YOU HAVE A BRAIN TUMOR." Wham, I turned on the judge and exclaimed, "Judge Grump, I have a brain tumor." And off I went back to university lockup.

"I won," I said to the nurses. "I'll be released soon enough." In a few days, Judge Grump's decision was delivered to me. It said I was not suicidal, not homicidal, but was acting strange enough to ruin my status in the business world. The judge claimed I suffered from rapid speech and sleepless nights, caused a violent patient to hit me and had no insight into what the psychiatrists said I had. He sentenced me to up to six months incarceration, and instructed the University psychiatrists that they could use neuroleptics to treat me (my heart sank)—but only after they proved I didn't have a brain tumor (my heart floated into the atmosphere).

The Voice had done it. The University was screwed, the psychiatrists were screwed. It was a Catch-22; the psychiatrists' very large and tender Achilles heel had been mangled! With simple elegance, The Voice set the trap for all psychiatry.

The rules of incarceration and neuroleptic treatment requires that all physical illnesses that could lead to a psych diagnosis be eliminated before the psych diagnosis can be confirmed. Unless a psych diagnosis can be substantiated, the "undiagnosed" patient retains his or her right to refuse medical diagnostic tests or treatment. It was a stalemate.

Six weeks later, after The Voice and I had finished our business, the University's psychiatrists appealed to Judge Grump to allow them to force me to have a CT scan of my head. The judge surely knew that if I really had a brain tumor he and the University were dead meat—so he refused. Then, as it turned out, the University began plotting to get rid of me.

But it didn't matter. In those six weeks spent incarcerated, The Voice and I had reached enlightenment.

Chapter 19: Life in the University Hospital Psych Ward

Being locked up freed me. I was free of my venture capital business, free of the usual household duties, free from taking out the garbage, cleaning the toilet, doing laundry, cleaning the cat box, shopping, planning meals. "Hey, Stephen," the sweet, innocent dietician would sing out every day. "Can I help you choose your nutritious, delicious, gourmet treats from today's menu?"

"You certainly can and come sit on my lap while I do so," I would fire back. I was also free of money worries as I had $20,000 in the bank and nowhere to spend it; free of shaving, getting haircuts, filling my car with gas, free of my children who had already left home—and best of all, free of those busybody psychiatrists. Free of their tests and inane inquiries, and free, thank heaven, of having to take their badass neuroleptics. I was free! Damned if The Voice hadn't pulled it off.

The psych ward had a specific rhythm. I took well to the three square meals a day and evening snack. I ate ravenously. Each morning I would compile a hit list of thirty or forty people to call. From the communal phone in the hallway I'd contact business associates, friends, relatives, offending psychiatrists and their wives, university hospital administrators, my lawyers, my children, Madelaine, Nick, the Minneapolis Star Tribune reporters, my mother.

To Madelaine, I'd say, "I am going to hound the shit out of you until you cough up my computer you bitch."

"You broke the answering machine, go to hell," she'd say. "Leave us alone."

Nick would only sputter. "You, you, you, you, you're crazy!!!!"

Various psychiatrists told me, "We're sorry, but it's for your own good." And, "Please don't harass my wife anymore!"

University administrators said, "No comment." Click.

A Star Tribune reporter was curt. "Yeah, I remember the article we did on your rural co-ops, how you were helping Native Americans and white trash get health care locally." When I tried to protest that I had never said that, they shut me down. "It doesn't matter what you did or didn't say. We aren't into publishing articles on kooks getting locked up by psychiatrists."

Some of my business associates seemed lost without me. One complained that, "The shorts are killing me. I'm two million shares long. You've got to help me; you got me into this mess!"

"Don't worry, The Voice will bail you out," I calmly told him. "What did you say? If the stock tanks below seven you'll be joining me in cuckoo land?" The stock price dropped down to five and my associate did crack like a brittle nut and did get locked up, but unfortunately not at the university with me.

To friends, I requested they come see me. "I have visiting hours from seven to ten. I have an opening at seven-thirty today. The shrinks are crazy. I've got them by the short hairs and they don't like it. False arrest."

I was blunt with my lawyers. "Why do I have to do all the work? Sue the university!"

To my mother, I defended myself, "Aha, so you've been in touch with my psychiatrists, and you think they should treat me. You want me to go along with their bullshit. No way. You'll see, they have it backwards. They're the crazies."

My dad just put me back on the phone with my mother. "I can't talk with you," he said, and I could hear the tears in his voice.

"You're crazy, get treatment," my sister said.

Then one day, a nurse stopped me. "You're cut off, no more phone calls," she said.

"Why?" I contentiously asked.

"This is the only phone for twenty patients and no one else can get a call in."

"Yeah, well none of these nuts wants to call out," I retorted.

"Well, if you really want to know the truth, people are complaining you're harassing the hell out of them and they want you cut off." My patient's rights advocate came in then, and wham! I was back in business. Apparently, I needed to be a lot more obnoxious to get booted off the phone permanently. God bless America! Through it all I can't say who was in charge of my phone campaign: The Voice or me?

With my days stretched out before me, I started exercising like a fiend. The psych ward was probably fifty yards long. Each day I walked back and forth at full speed for hours. I made about 200 round trips in a day, equal to ten miles. I would bang on the closed doors of other patients as I walked. "Who's there?" Or, "Huh?" Or, "Who knocked?" Or, "I didn't do anything," they'd call out from their rooms. What fun! On occasion, I would tackle the one exercise prop in the ward—a throwback stationary bike with a gauge that registered up to 100 whatevers. I'd feverishly peddle that gauge way past 100, threatening to blow the wheels off the relic.

I started to lose weight. Soon I went from a sluggish, 200 pounds to a slim,

trim 165.

The bathroom, with its urine-splattered toilet, was another way to pass the time. I got very good at hooking the toe of my shoe under the small amount of toilet seat that lipped over the toilet bowl and then lifting it to pee—a skill I still practice at public toilets.

About mid-incarceration my mother took ill, her chronic congestive failure worsening. This recurrent dilemma was most often brought on by her uncontrollable pastrami-philia. She was hospitalized near her home on the Jersey coast. Things quickly went from bad to worse. This was not the time for her to die, not while I was in lockup. I called her doctor to get a clearer understanding of what was going on. I had become extremely adroit at playing the middleman between my relatives and their doctors when the health chips were down. Her doctor was pessimistic. "Your mother's kidneys aren't working well at all. If we try to use diuretics to get the water off her lungs she could end up with kidney failure. We're caught between the devil and the deep blue—or yellow in this case—sea."

"Yes, that's probably true," I said. "But if you don't try to get the water off she certainly will die, and a miserable death at that. Give diuresis a try."

He refused, he argued with me, we were at loggerheads, I was losing him. Then suddenly The Voice spoke up. "TELL HIM TO GET A RENAL CONSULT."

Why didn't I think of that? Damned if The Voice wasn't brilliant. "The least you can do is get a renal consult," I told Mom's doctor. Sure enough, the deal was done. The kidney consultant worked Mother's kidneys like a plumber works a faucet. Her heart bounced back and she was sent home after having been proclaimed pastrami-worthy! The Voice had come through, again working a mini-miracle. My mother would live to see me "recover" my sanity, as far as she was concerned.

When I wasn't busy bothering people on the phone, eating, exercising, or BS-ing with my fellow kooks, I listened to The Voice. We were quite cozy at this point, and, with all that free time stretched out in front of us, we finally did the work we were supposed to get done at the psych ward country club.

Chapter 20: Revelation [1]

Before I had been committed, The Voice had already had me deal with my humanity, challenging me to figure out if I was good or evil. I lucked out: I was both, an average human. Now The Voice started our Psych Ward sessions with, "WHAT DO YOU THINK OF G-D?" Or asking me, "WHAT IS G-D?" The first thing that popped into my mind was Michelangelo's portrayal of G-d on the ceiling of the Sistine Chapel, touching his finger to Adam's, giving him the breath of life.

"Great painting, very inspirational," I said to The Voice. "But that's not G-d, that's a mighty distinguished-looking old Jewish man in great physical shape. In the Torah, G-d is a voice who talks to Adam and Eve, Noah, Abraham, and Moses, but who can also shake things up pretty seriously. He's a rough, demanding character we can't even see—or we die if we do." As I spoke, I realized I did not believe that the Torah's G-d was actually G-d to me.

"DIG DEEPER," The Voice encouraged.

I thought about it harder. "G-d must be something that's felt inside of me. A force. If it's in me it must be in everyone, and in animals too. Probably even in amoebas, otherwise how could they be so clever?"

The Voice and I decided to name this force The Blur, because, since it's only a feeling, the mind can't focus on it. I realized that it fit with the Old Testament belief that you can't look upon G-d or truly know the mind of G-d, but you can feel G-d. I finally understood those wondrous moments I had of pure joy that brought tears of love to my eyes, when I loved everyone in the world. If I were to die in those moments, I would have died joyously. Each moment was an epiphany, I realized. My experiences of epiphany must be that G-d force, The Blur welling up in me. I had learned at age fifty that epiphany in Christianity referred to the revelation of Christ. The date when it's celebrated is January 6th, my birthdate.

"But it must be coincidence and nothing more," I said to The Voice. "If G-d is in me, then he, she, *it* is in everyone, and maybe in everything."

"WHAT ABOUT EVIL?" The Voice inquired.

I answered, "If every living creature was filled with the G-d force, how could there be evil, a devil, hell? Maybe there's no such separate force as evil. Maybe evil is the inability to express the G-d force, the inability to express love or to have epiphanies."

The more I spoke, the more I believed my words. Here is a chance to get my name on a new medical syndrome, I thought. They could call it Zuckerman's Disorder or Impacted Love Syndrome (ILS). Loneliness, and the inability to feel for others, to love others, will be its hallmarks. Sufferers of ILS could do harm to others with impunity. Dickens hit the nail on the head in *A Christmas Carol*; Scrooge is a great case study of Impacted Love Syndrome. He has no feelings whatsoever for the harm he causes Bob Cratchit's family, especially to Tiny Tim, crippled from birth. A couple of harrowing nightmares featuring his former business partner, Jacob Marley, and the ghosts of Christmas past, present and future, prove cathartic. Love pours out of every one of Scrooge's pores. He is cured of his ILS.

The Voice impressed upon me that the Impacted Love Syndrome was a result of not being smothered in childhood by doting parents. Yes, I was lucky, and how I now wanted to love Helen and Max back for smothering me! All their deficiencies—smoking three packs of cigarettes a day, obesity, flaunting diabetic diets, their disruptive shouting matches, tortuous winner-take-all pinochle games, their anemic educational résumés—didn't amount to a hill of beans. They had loved the "hell" out of me and that's all that mattered.

The Voice didn't let up. "WHY WOULD G-D, LOVE, THE BLUR OR WHATEVER TRANSFORM ITSELF INTO THE PHYSICAL UNIVERSE? WHAT'S THE MOTIVE OF THIS CRIME?"

I couldn't help myself. "Strictly for entertainment," I glibly replied.

The Voice didn't chew me out for being audacious or simpleminded. As was its pattern of inquiry, it encouraged me to dig deeper, to plum my feelings. I found myself questioning why it seemed that every successful religion I knew of had G-d or the g-ds intermingling with humans, finding earthly women attractive and having all varieties of offspring with them, joining in human wars, and playing havoc with lives (we all know what Acts of G-d mean). Is it because heaven is boring? A lonely place? I realized that to me it isn't G-d Almighty, G-d the voyeur; it is G-d getting "its" kicks as the G-d of love, in us, with us. It was the G-d who travels the road of life with me, sharing moments of joy and sorrow, and, at moments of epiphany, G-d and I are inseparable, all love, life, and death a blur.

It was then that I felt I could sleep, knowing that I had finally discovered what The Voice was trying to tell me all along.

Chapter 21: Revelation 2

As The Voice and I proceeded, it began to feel as though I was having psychoanalysis performed on me. Freud must have had the same voice in his head as I had in mine. It wanted to know everything about my life and especially inquired about my family relationships: my father and mother, and my two siblings, my sister Bernice and young brother Bobby.

I told The Voice everything about my family and upbringing. It wasn't your typical patriarchal unit. My mother was the wearer of the pants, the strong-armed stoic in the family. But that didn't stop her outward histrionics, which misled people into thinking she was weak. In reality, her tears were crocodile tears; her fits of exaltation and anguish were engrossing theatrics.

How I loved, as a 10-year-old, watching my mother host her women's poker gang for Wednesday night coffee and cards. My mother, Helen, infused the goings-on with emotion and cunning. "A draw like this never happens. How could I win with a pair of deuces? Dumb luck, I suppose. Next time you'll draw aces," she'd say, even as she won again and again. Every Thursday morning, I would demand to know how much she had won the evening before: $5.40, $6.10, or $12.50. She'd be tired—the game didn't end until around 1 a.m.—and I often had to make my own breakfast while she slept in. Still, she would always find the time to regale me with stories about her tricks and score-keeping techniques.

Needless to say, I was proud of my mom! To be a winner every time took skill, intelligence, manipulation, bluffing. She had it all. I would brag, in later years, that my mom, the card shark, paid for my medical school tuition out of her poker winnings. It wasn't entirely untrue, either.

Besides card sharking, Mother was also the neighborhood's philosopher of basic emotional survival in a world fraught with uncertainty. "Peace and quiet. Six feet under." Or, "Don't believe anything you hear and only half of what you see," she would often say. She was armed with 4,000 years of Jewish homilies. If the devil himself had made an appearance before Helen, he wouldn't have elicited much more than a shrug, and a "What took you so long?"

My father, for all his street smarts honed by a lifetime in the *schmatte* business in Manhattan's Garment District, was the softie when it came to family. This included his crew of multiracial workers at his various dress manufacturing businesses. I can only remember one occasion, when I was eight or nine, when he tried to discipline me. In a fit of anger he dragged me by my arm upstairs to my bedroom. I feared a beating, but how? He had never beaten me in the past. Once in my bedroom he let me go and burst into sobbing tears. He then left my room without a word. How I loved that man, though always at a distance. But that was true of both my parents, particularly as time went on. The more schooling I had, the more estranged I became from the world I had grown up in.

"You've got a day off from school," my dad said to me. "Come up with me to see the business." Did he want me to inherit his *schmatte* business? Nah; he only wanted me to be proud of him. He also clearly wanted to show me off to his employees, the doctor-to-be. "Meet Edwardo, he's the king of shipping," my dad would say in a typical encounter. "Edwardo, meet my son Stephen. He wants to be a doctor." I'd shake hands with Edwardo. "Edwardo is the best, you should see him in traffic on

36th Street with a cart loaded with dresses." Dad would then steer me to the next person. "Hey, Manelo, meet my son, show him how the cutting table works."

"You're going to be a doctor? You're not going into the dress business? My son is going to school to be an engineer," Manelo proudly revealed. It was a theme among my father's workers—every immigrant wanted their son to have a prominent profession, one that wasn't tied to the *schmatte* business. Manelo was Italian, but it was something he innately had in common with my father, the Jew.

All my dad's half dozen or so dress businesses—one bad season and you declared bankruptcy and opened a new company—were in the same building: 525 7th Avenue. It was on Fashion Ave, one block north of Macy's flagship store on 34th Street. Each floor in the building usually had three *schmatte* manufacturers whose names were listed on the floor's registry: Alice Reed, Beverly Fashions, Missy Fashions, and so on. "This is the showroom for buyers. The models aren't here now," my dad would say. There was always the suspicion that my dad may have been *schtupping* a model or two. When this line of gossip reached my mother, she would, in her indubitable fashion, dismiss the accusations with: "He comes home at night with his paycheck."

The Voice asked a lot about my parents, but seemed pretty much happy with my relationship with my sister. She was four years older than me, and a child prodigy at clothing design. She wasn't much interested in academics, however, or in getting a college education. She was always a mother-like figure to me, and remains so up to today. Both she and my mother provided me with that special brand of love that only a mother can give a child.

My brother, seven years younger, looked up to me. He clearly thought I was hot stuff—sometimes to my annoyance. When I was thirteen and he six years old, I caught the largest fish I had to date—a five pound bass. Twenty years later, we talked about that day and he remembered everything: the sun reflecting on the water, the way the fish fought against the line. My own memory paled in comparison to his. He also used to follow my friends and I around, paying close attention to who I was friendly with that week. *Get a life*, I often thought. But I couldn't really fault him. That's what younger brothers do—they idolize their older brothers. Still, the attention bothered me; I was brought up

Jewish and I didn't want to bear the burden of idolhood. In time, much to my liking, I became a broken idol, no longer a god, but "just" a brother to Bobby. I was much happier with our relationship as we aged, and it didn't even bother me that he had conspired to get me locked up in the University Psych Ward. If he hadn't, all the wild and necessary stuff wouldn't have happened. After all, it was an act of love. Why would he do it except to try and save me?

None of my nuclear family and I seemed to have any big unresolved issues or stumbling blocks to our ongoing relationships. In truth, we were a rather normal down-to-earth bunch. Maybe even a little boring. Still, The Voice wanted to hear all about them, and I was glad to dive into our histories together.

Because most of my family lived in the New York area or beyond, visits from them while I was locked up were infrequent. We did talk often by phone however, a communication tool I became a champ at using. And while my family couldn't come by very often, there were many friends who did visit me under the unusual circumstances I was in. I have no doubt they came for my benefit—though I'm also sure that they were curious about what had come over me. Was I mad? Did I deserve to be under lock and key?

One day, a week into my lock up, a ward nurse pushed my door open. "You have a visitor," she said. "A mister Harold Jester."

"Harold! How are things on the outside?" I greeted him with. We never did get to discuss HDII, the company we both sat on the board of. Rather, Harold wanted to know how The Voice and I were getting on. I unloaded on him, because I knew he truly wanted me to and that he believed in the prophetic nature of my voice. He wasn't disappointed, and neither was I. Our conversation transcended the setting, the lockup psych ward. By the end, we both concurred that there was a loving force in the universe.

My colleague and friend Sid Stein also showed up. We avoided discussing his role in getting his psychiatrist friend to lock me up on a 72-hour hold. Like my brother, I had no animosity for his part in my confinement. He was a participant in the drama, not a cause of it.

"How brilliant you are," he exclaimed just before he left our visit. I assumed he said this in regard to The

Voice trapping the psychiatry department by urging me to say I had a brain tumor—which indeed was a brilliant coup. When I asked him to elaborate, he only smiled and took his leave.

"How are the crazies treating you?" my next guest, Dr. Mike, inquired. Dr. Mike was both a good friend and an outlier, not unlike me. He was born into a surgical family of Mayo Clinic aristocracy. Mike was third generation, though if there ever was an ill fit in the lineage, he was it. He bounced from orthopedic surgery residency to training as a radiologist to practicing as a family practitioner before finally landing in psychiatry. His meandering smacked of a life of happenstance. It was easy to talk to Dr. Mike about The Voice, incarceration, being deemed insane. The parochial view of insanity that had gotten me locked up was not his. In reality, I wasn't sure which of my friends and family deemed me "crazy" at that point.

My psychiatrist, the one I had hired, certainly didn't. My lawyers didn't think so either. They didn't even send me a bill, trusting that I would honor their eventual payment. The friends and associates who visited or called didn't seem to think so either, many asking for my advice. My family, on the other hand, was clearly concerned about my mental status. But they were also being prompted by the University psychiatrists.

I didn't feel crazy, and my sanity seemed clearer the longer I stayed locked up. Could it be that the University psychiatry department and the hospital administration had become so committed to branding me with a diagnosis that retreating from their position would be embarrassing, or worse, make them vulnerable to legal action? At first I thought it couldn't be possible. These were the people who claimed to have my best interests at heart. But what followed made this line of reasoning seem more and more likely.

"Dr. so and so wants to meet with you," the ward nurse proclaimed one day.

"Who the hell is she? I don't recognize that name." I answered.

"She is the head of Adult Psychiatry. Should I tell her it's okay?"

"Why not?" I answered. I was curious, a bit flattered, and The Voice didn't raise any objections.

The department head and I met informally, in the living room area of the psych ward. At first we made polite chit chat. "How are you doing in here?" she finally asked me.

"If you really want to know, I have a problem," I said. "Your guys want to treat me with neuroleptics. Frightening drugs, with horrible side effects! You really need to stop using them."

Though she protested, there was no attempt at counseling or manipulation to solve the contentious stalemate between her department's players and The Voice (or, me). I felt she had come mainly to see for herself this exotic bird that had alighted in her backyard. Or maybe there was a more sinister motive I did not perceive, regardless of how cordially our meeting ended.

Then, one day, out of the blue, I sensed my conservations with The Voice were about to end. There seemed to be no more issues to discuss. The thought that this was it, that The Voice would go silent, its work done, greatly saddened me. My wondrous, brilliant mentor would be no more. "You are going to leave me and I don't want you to," I told The Voice that day.

"HOW CAN I LEAVE YOU?" The Voice responded. "I AM YOUR VOICE. Now we have merged, your inner voice and your outer voice. You no longer have a need for me to speak to you in your deaf ear. I am you. I have been and always will be with you. The time to converse is over. Now is the time to act on what you have learned. Before you were you, but you did not know it. Now you know who you are."

I knew without question that what The Voice said was true. Over the past four months I had grown from fear, to fondness, to love of The Voice. And now the greatest revelation had come upon me: The Voice was my voice, my inner subconscious voice, my intuitive self, G-d in me. I had fallen in love with myself!

But who was "myself?" Had The Voice—the force in me—really taken me over? Was I just a do-good pawn? Maybe. But despite all of The Voice's imponderable knowledge and insight, it was still my inner voice I had heard, utterly unique to me; so there must be some "me" in there too. I do think I have free will, even if it didn't always feel that way. In any case, I was just thrilled to know The Voice was in me, *is* me. In the end, that was all that mattered.

Shortly after The Voice went silent, the plot thickened. Early one morning, two Sheriff's deputies stormed into my bedroom unannounced, handcuffed me, threw my few possessions into a cardboard box, and led me criminal-style out of the University Psych Ward. I was warned not to resist; I was too scared to anyway.

At first I had no idea where I was being taken. As we drove north, my captors became friendlier and let on that we were headed for the Brainerd State Psychiatric Hospital. My dual-site commitment included either the University Psychiatric Ward or Anoka State Hospital. Anoka was full. Brainerd State, where I had been a consultant in the past, had a few openings, so that's where we were headed. The University psychiatrists had had enough of me. Even with all my connections to the university, they wanted me out and badly. Letting me go free was not an option. Never informing my lawyers, they shanghaied me to the state's brutal inpatient mental health system.

At Brainerd State, the rules changed quickly. Now I was in for *One Flew Over the Cuckoo's Nest*-style bedlam, the real world of psychiatric institutionalization in America.

Chapter 22: Asylum

Where the University Psych Ward was welcoming and filled with light, Brainerd was dark and prison-like. My first five days there sent me into a tailspin; The Voice was gone, and I suffered overwhelming drug-induced anxiety that didn't allow me a moment's respite. I fed my body in five-minute forced spurts, afraid of starving but unable to alight for a second longer. I hobbled about my prison corridors in a daze. I lay down a thousand times, only to toss and turn in agony. At some point I hit critical mass and my sweat-drenched body frantically righted itself. Fatigued beyond fatigue, I pulled on my clothes, shoes, and socks and, once again, thrust myself into the openness of the shadowy corridors.

The incessant anxiety drove me to pace my confinement—down Corridor A, the Suicide Protection Unit—through the blue fumes of the Smokers' Inferno, where bleary-eyed, lobotomized puffers hid in its smoky recesses. On to Corridor B, rank with the piss-stench of communal toilets. Beyond the stark four-bed dormers strewn with other prisoners. Past the cloudy surveillance mirror, where I watched a reflection that barely looked like me head in the opposite direction. On to the padded lockup room that marked the end of my pilgrimage and the beginning of my next revolution. The only relief from my nerve-jangling fits was from the twenty to thirty cold showers I took daily, dutifully charted in my dossier by the nursing wardens. And so it went again and again.

I existed. Period. My mind was choked with mandatory medication and involuntary exhaustion. My bedroom was filled with the stifling August heat and three menacing strangers who were also newly imprisoned and besieged by ominous tomorrows.

Like me, my cellmate, Nervous Cat, performed his own yo-yo-like ritual. He'd fling himself violently onto his cot, thrash about amidst his sheets, kick his locker, and then curse himself into a frenzy. With no warning he'd bolt upright and disappear down Corridor A, dressed only to the waist, to vent his rage in the Smoker.

My other two roommates were barely visible. We communicated to one another in grunts and gestures, each of us recently trapped, caged, and helpless. Our four bare cots were adorned with black-striped mattresses of two-inch thickness, a coarse pillow, a sheet that no one bothered using and a thin cotton blanket. Every cot had a set of matching rickety, green metal lockers, battered by previous inmates—perhaps in hopes that someone would remember them. We also had crude, waist-high dressers with four sticky drawers and no mirror. Two large windows, sans drapes, welcomed the summer's swelter. They wouldn't open, but were instead adorned with thin transoms to prevent suffocation. This was my "personal" space while in captivity.

Prior to my transfer to Brainerd State Hospital, the University psychiatrists made a final appeal to Minnesota's Attorney General and won. His signature erased my human rights. Soon after I arrived at Brainerd, I was held down by six aids, injected with a sedative and forced through a CAT scan to prove that my brain tumor was a hoax—which, of course, it was. I wondered how many of them would have denied their actions under penalty of perjury if I had later taken them to court. But for now, like all prisoners, I was forced to accept that the system held all the cards.

After the "no-tumor-found" CAT scan, I was put on the multi-drug neuroleptic cocktail that was in vogue at the time. Thus began my crazed perambulations. Even though they severely impaired my thinking, I still had the wherewithal to know I would die unless my medications were changed or stopped. I wasn't wrong. Not long after they started the medications, I collapsed and was rushed to the area medical hospital with a toxic reaction.

My medications were adjusted, but the toxic pacing continued. I still knew I had to persuade the rarely visible wizard of our Oz—Dr. Walter—into changing my drugs or stopping them altogether. I knew he wouldn't agree to stop them, but if he didn't change my cocktail it was only a matter of time before I crashed again. I waited in ambush for him, obsequiously badgering his nurses on his whereabouts within the hospital. Was he even here yet? Was he in a meeting? Would he be here by 3 p.m.? Why was he delayed? Was he screwing that big-breasted blond nurse in the consultation room? I worked them over daily, but it only seemed to fuel their disdain for me as some annoying, disenfranchised creature. I tempered my own anger until it became a white glow in the middle of my brain, determined that the day would come when I would ensnare Dr. Walter and this infernal, inhuman monster-machine of psychiatric incarceration. One day, I knew I'd try to destroy it. But for now, guerrilla warfare was my only available tactic. If I bit the monster directly on the neck, it would label me untreatable. Then it could crush me with more drugs, solitary confinement, shock therapy, and more lock up.

I finally succeeded in cornering Dr. Walter, who listened to my pleadings for all of thirty seconds and decided to change my medications. But to what? The new mix was none of my business, according to the nurses. After all, I was incapable of any rational comprehension.

Four times a day, the announcement blared out: "Medication time!" All of us inmates lined up dutifully, like well-behaved zombies, for drugs at the tellers' windows. Only then would we know if our medications had been changed. Not because the nurses told us, but because the pills and capsules changed color and shape, and the liquids changed color, odor, viscosity.

I balked at being forced to swallow the unknown drugs and I crossed an invisible line by asking too many questions. "What is this blue pill, this green liquid?" I'd ask. The drug teller's face read *shut up and swallow* as she tersely rattled off the names of a half dozen psych meds. Being a doctor, I knew exactly what they were pumping into my body. But when I objected, the teller acted insulted and threatened to call the guards, who would gladly force my medication on me.

How I dreaded swallowing those numerous toxins that had caused me all forms of psychological and physiological aberrations! Once downed, the "side effects" were unavoidable. In truth, they weren't side effects at all, but the effects of poison. I had adapted, somewhat, to the debilitation of my previous drug regime, but now, I braced myself for new horrors. Fortunately, after talking to Walter I was put on a concoction that was less devastating. The anxiety, the pacing, and the showers all stopped.

After surviving my drug ordeal, I searched for a way out. Day after day, I beseeched my social worker, Tom Kingbird, to clarify my status. He was a "busy man," which meant, in his limited vocabulary, that a mere stroke of his pen could cause me either great harm or good. The g-ds of the asylum listened to him so Tom was in a safe position to execute favors or punishments at whim.

In the end, Tom Kingbird turned out to be one of "us." He'd been locked up at one time and had returned to the system to milk it for dough and power. He now had the best of all worlds, considering the blows life had dealt him as an alcoholic who'd been deemed "crazy" to boot. Tom knew the system inside and out. In many ways he was the embodiment of the system's erratic use of power. But I found that he generally kept his word when he gave it.

I begged Tom for a transfer to Sector B, and got it.

My new room faced north. The summer sun no longer inflamed my bed. Best of all my new roommates were old timers who'd calmly settled into the horror with savvy and without guilt. My new *compadres*.

These new roommates taught me the art of "mouthing" pills so I could spit them out later. They taught me about radios and tape players and how to hustle our keepers to get the batteries needed to play them. They showed me the secrets of getting smokes day or night, how to protect your coffee stash, who to share it with, how to tap hot water from a myriad of out-of-bounds faucets and—most vitally—how one should act if caught. In short, they taught me how to retain my humanity while trapped in the belly of the monster.

In time, I too began to frequent the Smoker, and, although not a smoker myself, I adjusted to the dimly lit languid smoke-filled terrain of our den of inequity. Layer upon layer, the yellow walls were stained nicotine brown. The eight foot around, rough-hewn tables and the scraped, scarred, and slashed Salvation Army chairs were scattered in clusters. A myriad of ashtrays sat on the tables and the floor, always full of ashes, butts, and spittle. At the head of the Smoker stood two wooden rectangular tables under the naked glare of ceiling lights that cast shadows into the grimy recesses of the large room.

The head tables accommodated the employees in charge of maintaining decorum in the Smoker. They doled out cigarettes to momentarily abate the incessant cravings of the inmates. One cigarette per customer per 15 minutes, 24 hours a day. The line established itself just before the quarter-hour and the employees regularly shortchanged the clock to avoid being nagged. I supposed it was also a gesture of good will.

The rights to cigarettes were obtained in a variety of ways that included exchanging your disability welfare check for your favorite brand, being a beneficiary of the covert founder of the cigarette endowment fund, guilting what family and friends still recognized your existence, theft, and, above all, mooching. The cigarette cult permeated our society-in-exile and the Smoker was its capital.

Even in crazy captivity there was a woman: Sally. She and I began holding intriguing meetings in the Smoker where we held hands, shared butts, kissed, and fondled each other in the dingy shadows. Sally denied the existence of my fondling, later pretending she hadn't let me put my hand up her shirt or along her thigh. With a lean, poised body, short curly blond hair, darting clear blue eyes, and subtle breasts, she entertained herself by playacting a fear of being defiled by men. Her mind was seeded with paranoia. Her gig was to call men of power who she picked out of the phonebook. Lawyers, doctors, CEOs—she called at all hours, demanding they secure her freedom. When anyone would listen, she spent each call recanting the poisonous drugs that had been foisted on her, describing how they were eating at her brain, inflaming her gut. A sexy child-woman, over-medicated, frightened, and pushy, she was beyond even electro-shock.

*

It's two in the morning and all is well in the Smoker. John has his headset radio scattered all over the large round wooden table and is attempting to black-tape repair its bare guts. For four dollars, he'd just bought twenty dollars' worth of radio from a new incarcerate. Fixing, breaking, re-fixing. He'd bought the whole package: waist-attached tape players with headphone privacy; the prized cassette tapes; an army of batteries, double AA, alkaline, triple AAA. Some used, some new, some no good at all. Barter, borrow, buy, cache away for the needy day.

I too am a member of the electronic music subculture with my own cassette player and headphones. My prize recording: Berlioz's "Symphonie fantastique." How utterly sublime to dance through my prison's corridors, past the Smoker and its puffing patrons, while secretly tuned in to what only I can hear.

Randy postures out of the gloom, ostensibly to help John but we all know better. Randy's air of monotonous superiority is more boring than offensive, even, at times, a bit entertaining. John won't give in to Randy's attempt to dominate; rather he collects the pieces of his electronic world and leaves. There will always be another day. Randy banters on and points his fingers, sermonizing on the need for order and rules or bragging that his myriad of contacts on the "outside" are waiting to take him in. He then parades proudly up to the head table and preaches at the employees doling out the cigarettes to provoke, ingratiate or simply relieve his boredom. But they are just as accustomed to his biteless bark and even admire him as they would a peacock.

John is an economic disaster to the monster. A hundred and fifty thousand dollars out of the system's wallet and at age thirty-five, John still has $500,000 to go. He is also the sweetest, brightest, and most caring soul I have met in a long time. I don't believe that his off-base Rube Goldberg-esque inventions are a sign of what got him institutionalized, but rather the result of twenty-two years of drugs and institutionalization. Often, he launches into a tirade that lacerates drug psychiatry. "None of this shit works," he says, because he "ain't really sick." But he revels in his theory that he is blowing the hell out of the state's mental health budget, killing them as they are trying to kill him.

I am often fully entertained and pleasantly distracted by John's lectures on bizarre, erudite articles, published by the psychiatric towers of Babel. Psychiatry still preaches success through correct labeling within their 280 categories. Matching each category are drug regimens that attempt to create a post-Haight-Ashbury paradiso: Haldol, LSD, Prozac, Hash, Thorazine, mescaline. John and I are caught in our own regime at Brainerd, but not so drugged up that we can't comprehend the neat psychiatric boxes they are trying to fit us into.

One day, Sally tells me she is getting out soon, to be returned to her drunken, abusive father. "Can I stay at your house? Won't you take care of me?" she begs. Sure I will. Just give me $50,000 a year and a social worker who actually cares. But the reality is that there is no funding to be found, and that I can't take on Sally even if I wanted to. No, Sally will be doomed to institutionalization until the monster is slain and rational treatment for humans with emotional disturbances are invented. Right now, it is easier to lock her up and drug her: out of sight, out of mind.

One day, Sally disappears. Word is she's been discharged. No one thought to inform her friends—who are we, anyway? But she is back in a week with fresh tales of mistaken identities, demonic psychiatrists, drug blackouts, and a new pair of cowboy boots that accentuate her slender sexiness. Our romance resumes its former function: a calming background noise that allows her to obsess on the brain damage she senses is slowly, invisibly enveloping her. She is terrified that the drugs are permanently "fixing" her. And they probably are, but I am too preoccupied with her breasts to be anything other than an agreeable sounding board.

Then it happens. A fellow inmate rats on me. I am caught spitting out, into the communal toilet, the very elixir of mental health my saviors deem will right me—a major assault on the system. I can no longer be trusted. My credibility, already at an all-time low, tumbles to zero. "Open your mouth," the attendant threateningly orders and with a flashlight in hand she searches my oral cavity four times a day, looking for stowed away pills.

John has begun to posture, his body becoming contorted, his arms and hands askew. He takes a step and then re-postures. Another step, another re-posture. With his wicked sense of humor, I mistake this for a new parody he is creating. But I suddenly realize that it is the tradive dyskinesia of Haldol. His face becomes fixed in a grimace, to which he adds a sardonic flare. Seasoned by my own suffering, I convince him to mouth his poison and advise him on how to avoid my fate—use the water fountains; avoid the toilets with their prying eyes.

John has already informed the doctors about his previous problems with Haldol, but this is the world of which Kafka wrote. Orders are issued from The Great Oz, who may or may not have read John's chart, who may have erred but is beyond reproof, and whose capriciousness always wreaks havoc. John learns to mouth his Haldol, recovers, and balance is restored.

Life in Building One goes on—its inhabitants, myself included, trying to piece together shredded selves into some form of supportive society in captivity. All the while, our keepers fight a stiffly organized resistance against our need to belong. I grope for love, for kindness, for hope—blurred as I am—instinctually drawn to this community of comrades.

The time comes when I am expendable. The system does not need me any longer. It had justified incarceration, justified diagnosis, justified druggings, and finally, justified disgorgement. Ironically, the admonishment I receive upon being vomited from the belly of the beast is, "Don't come back!" Almost all do, again and again. My prognosis is "guarded," a polite medical term for "hopeless."

*

And just like that, I was sent out from my sheltered world, away from my comrades, and was folded into the darkest cocoon of my mind where I lost nearly all hope of being me again.

Chapter 23: Early Fall, 1991

How I got from Brainerd State Hospital to my home in Minneapolis is still a mystery to me. Was it by bus, a taxi, or some state owned transportation vehicle for lost souls with no one to greet them on discharge? I don't remember. But I do remember the gloom that settled over me when I arrived in the dark of evening to a shrouded house.

Dick, my boarder, had moved out of his basement apartment two months before, but he dutifully came every week to check on my mail, to see if the house had been burglarized or burned to the ground, to make sure the lawn got mowed so the neighbors wouldn't report any unkempt conditions. He always turned off all the house lights when he finished his duties.

After months of constant activity and being surrounded by fellow inmates and caretakers day and night, suddenly there was nothing: no one at home, no work to arouse me in the morning, no family around to comfort me. The rug of my asylum society was pulled out from under me. Being released was what I wanted, but I never anticipated what my emancipation would lead to. I felt naked and truly alone. What came to mind was the suicide of Decoud in Joseph Conrad's *Nostromo*. Decoud's utter isolation, his emptiness, leads him to extinguish his already diminished flame of life. But while we shared similarities, I was not Decoud. I clung to the thin thread of belief that I would recover.

Instead of suicide, my days were consumed by extreme panic attacks. In the hours where I wasn't curled in a ball, sweating and shaking, I reorganized my house. I shuffled furniture about, decluttered, and threw away years of accumulation in an attempt to wash away the past by giving me something seemingly worthwhile to do in the present.

One week after my release from Brainerd, I drove to Brooklyn Center to visit my social worker. Her office was in a convenient shopping mall, easy to locate. The planned appointment gave me a reason to get up, get out. That's how bad things had gotten.

"How are you doing, Stephen?" My social worker, Ami, cheerfully asked as soon as we were sitting in her office.

"Horrible. I have nonstop anxiety."

Less cheerful and more businesslike, Ami nodded. "Maybe you should join a manic depressive group. I can arrange that. Have you seen a psychiatrist since your discharge?"

"No, but I have an appointment with Dr. Abzhanova in three days."

"Good, make sure you keep the appointment. I'll make an appointment for you to see me again in a month."

Desperation enveloped me. My upcoming appointment with Dr. Abzhanova was a slender bird of hope. The reputable doctor was known far and wide for his wizardry at mastering the confounding myriad of anti-depressant chemicals fed to his patients. His office waiting room hummed with the silence of the depressed multitudes waiting their turn at chemical redemption. Finally, it was my turn.

Again: "How are you doing, Stephen?"

"Not well," I admitted. "I stopped the discharge medications that Dr. Walter put me on. They didn't work. I can't sleep and I'm anxious all the time."

"Then let's try another medication for your depression," Dr. Abzhanova proclaimed in a positive tone of voice. "I've written this prescription for a thirty day supply. Make an appointment to see me in a month."

Goodbye. Next. The seven-minute generic visit was over. Flop goes the wizard. I didn't make another appointment to see Dr. Abzhanova, nor did I fill the prescription he gave me.

Day after day, I hid in my house, afraid to go out. Finally, in desperation, I managed to find the courage to call an old friend.

"Marshall, can I come visit you today?" I asked over the phone. "Maybe even stay the night?"

Marshall was an extroverted bachelor who had long been a father figure to me. We met when he was the hospital administrator in the down-on-its-luck town of Onamia, located in central Minnesota. A town the railroad built and then forgot. He'd recruited me to doctor in his rural community after my internal medicine residency at the University of Minnesota had ended.

Fresh out of training and full of ideas and ideals, Marshall helped me start up a rural medical co-op that would hopefully change the world for the better. For ten years, the rural co-op Marshall and I founded did just that, weaving urban specialists and educators into the fabric of rural healthcare. "What you have created is a network," my Berkeley sociologist buddy explained. "It's a new concept in organizational structure." I was relieved to hear that what I created now had a name and boundaries, goals that could be measured to determine its success or failure.

I often stayed over at Marshall's cabin on Mille Lacs Lake when making the rounds of the co-op communities. Marshall was my North Star when it came to navigating my desire to help those in need. His passion for the underdog never dimmed. He was a severe hypertensive, but he wouldn't let doctors treat him. Once we became close, he let me take a look at him, treat him, even save him from the fate of his father and brother: death by age fifty-five of heart attacks. Marshall eventually retired, sold his cabin, and moved into an apartment in Minneapolis.

When I called him during those dark days, he was as gracious as ever. "Sure, come for dinner, Steve, and feel free to stay over. I have a cot we can open up for you, though I've only got Hamburger Helper for dinner. Is that okay?"

"You bet it is."

At dinner, we got into it. *What happened to Daryl Gunderson? Was he still practicing in Onamia or did the Board finally suspend his license? Poor fellow, he was always paranoid as hell! Was Sister Claire still in hillbilly county in Appalachia? Did you ever hear from her? Did Art Garbo still represent the Vineland Reservations on the Hospital Board? How is Pearl doing after Steve's death?*

On and on we talked.

Later in the evening, Marshall finally broached the question I knew had been on his mind since I made my desperate call earlier that day. "What's wrong? What happened to you?"

It was a relief to unload it all. I told him about The Voice, my stay in the University Psych Ward, my Brainerd State ordeal. I described my current days and how I had fallen into a state of anxiety and suffered from panic attacks. The more I talked, the more a strange thing was happening. I started speaking with swagger, hyperbole, with humor. My anxiety was gone.

My intimacy with Marshall had transformed me. I was me again.

It was wonderful.

"Help me open the cot," Marshall requested as the evening wound down. After doing so, he went and pulled bedding from a closet. We made up the cot with a pillow, two sheets, and a thin but sufficient blanket.

"Thank you, Marshall. See you in the AM." I was still riding high on the euphoria of opening up to an old friend, but as soon as I lay down, the worms began to creep in.

You haven't got a job, and soon you'll be out of money. You won't be able to go back to practice; it's been seventeen years since you last did! All your relatives live in New York; even your children live elsewhere. Marshall is your only friend. You're too afraid to return to your house. You have to get Marshall to let you stay with him!

The switch had flipped back; I was having another panic attack. What had happened? How could I go from depressed to manic and back again so quickly? I tossed and turned the rest of the night.

"Good morning." I said to Marshall the next day. "Would it be okay for me to stay with you for a week or two? I can't go back to my house. I'm scared. I know it's a lot to ask."

"Are you suicidal?" he asked.

"No, though maybe I should be."

"I wish I could help, Steve," he said. "But this problem is too much for me. You need help."

I knew Marshall was right, yet I couldn't help but grasp at straws. I packed my bundle of jangled nerves and headed home.

I started going to the manic depressive group that my social worker found for me. There were six of us, and we'd meet in one member's house. Four of the members were women, one with memorably sexy legs. I was the only one not taking some sort of pill, some kind of drug. I felt somewhat like a voyeur, superior to these "lifers," who would never escape their mental prisons. They were their conditions, their diagnoses, where I assumed I would somehow go back to being normal. The question was how and when it would happen. Maybe I also didn't want to admit how much I had in common with my fellow group members, or how much I feared that I might not ever go back to "normal."

I quickly hit it off with an African American woman in the group. She was about my age, attractive, talkative, and educated. Her problem with depression began, she claimed, when she developed cataplexy and narcolepsy. I'd never heard of anyone with both conditions. Because of her diagnosis, she was banned from trial law, even though she had passed the bar. She eked out a meager living from the few law clients she had. Her apartment was a one-bedroom affair just off downtown Minneapolis and two blocks from the Mississippi River. She opened her heart to me, clearly recognizing that I was the more crippled one. "You can come live with me. I know my apartment is small, but we can work it out!"

I thought seriously about living with Ariadne, but I didn't want to be sexually involved and I felt this would inevitably become a problem. But she wasn't the only one who saw that I was drowning; my sister in New Jersey, with her large, empty house, with her big sister attitude, also offered to take me in. I was frightened at the idea of uprooting myself, of taking a flight where my anxieties might cause me to freak out. What would happen if I had a panic attack on the plane? The thought was terrifying.

Dan was a psychologist I had dealt with—and liked—when I was in the throes of divorce from my first wife. In desperation, I sought his advice. "Go to your sister's," he said, "but make plans to return to Minnesota when you're better." I took his advice, screwed up my courage to buy a one-way ticket to Newark Airport and boarded the plane. I needed to get out. If I didn't go to my sister's in New Jersey, I was seriously thinking of turning myself back in to Brainerd State—maybe never to leave this time.

My sister's house in ritzy Holmdel was large and sat on a half-acre of property. She had a pool in her backyard that was covered over since it was already October. I was relegated to her spare bedroom and her whims. "Get out of bed and have breakfast!" she'd say in the morning. "Don't go back to sleep, I'm making an appointment for you to see a psychiatrist. If you don't go there, you can at least get out of the house and volunteer at the hospital."

My anxiety had manifested into sickening waves of pain that pierced the left side of my belly. I was in pain all day long, and all I wanted to do was lay in bed. "I can't take this!" I would whisper to myself after my sister had finished making her demands. But I recognized that I had no choice, and I got out of bed.

Not long after I arrived, my sister arranged an evening meeting with a psychiatrist. The woman worked during the day at a state psychiatric hospital presumably similar to Brainerd State and could only see me afterhours in an office that was several townships away from my sister's house. The parking lot of the complex was empty and the lights in the two-story building were all seemingly out. My sister and I walked down a dark corridor until we reached Room 202. When we knocked, a soft voiced called out, "Come in!"

At the end of a large, dimly-lit room sat a diminutive white-haired lady. Once again, I heard: "How are you doing, Stephen?" But this time I knew it wouldn't be a quick, seven-minute meeting.

The little psychiatrist was a mixture of old and new school, of psychoanalysis and psychiatry by drugs. She immediately did two wonderful things for me. She gave me Pamelor, an old-line tricycle anti-depressant, which, on the very first day I took it, quelled my stomach pains. Then she said to me, "It will take about one year for you to return to your old self," with such an assuring motherly voice, with such matter-of-factness, that I believed her.

New Jersey was full of action. I mustered up enough courage to go with my sister to a singles party in the next township. Somehow, I overcame my fright to make a move on a blonde ten of about thirty years of age, who was coolly talking to an older woman. She was agreeable, we danced, we tried to talk. Of all things, she was a nurse at a nearby hospital.

The conversation was fine, but something didn't feel right. It was like she wasn't all there. Then came the confession: "I was diagnosed two years ago with schizophrenia. I take Haldol to keep me under control." The ten was a two in personality, a complete zombie. I wondered how she could possibly be a nurse, as drugged up as she was.

Her older friend was more upbeat and took a shine to me. We even went on a date, chaperoned by my sister, to the famous English Town Flea Market. The Market was only open on weekends, its myriad of stalls filled with everything under the sun. Philly, my uncle by marriage to my father's younger sister, Lena, had a fish stall there. He was also the family's only known "over user" of alcohol. Every Saturday and Sunday he would drive his truck loaded with smoked fish delicacies to English Town at six in the morning to set up his stall. The smell was overwhelming, permeating Philly, his truck, and the stall. It was so bad that I half believed him when he claimed he only drank to deaden the odor of smoked fish.

My date didn't go well. For a while, I lost the lady in home appliances. When we were together, it wasn't much better; I didn't find her at all sexually alluring and I found her stories boring. Still, a date was a date, a step in the direction of recovery.

My visit to a manic-depression group meeting was much more rewarding. There must have been twenty of us kookies all sitting in a classroom together. A speaker welcomed us and gave a brief description of what the group was about—a chance to meet others with similar problems and to learn from them.

I hit it off with Anna, one of the members. Anna was four years younger than me, 5'2", with a kind face and a non-descript, slightly overweight body. She was sincere and bright. Two weeks before we met she had attempted suicide, overdosed on her sedative medication, and ended up on life support in the hospital.

Her failed suicide wasn't a cry for help—she meant it. Her second husband, the "love of her life" and a mentally deranged musician, had recently left her after five years of marriage and moved to California. He told her that their relationship was "driving him crazy and freaking him out." From her perspective they were still in love, but living with her had become toxic to him. He had to leave or else.

At age twenty-two, Anna had been "married off" by her Italian Catholic family to a prominent suitor whom she never loved and by whom she had two children. While still married, she met and fell desperately in love with the musician, eventually abandoning her husband, her children, her parents, and her siblings. The second marriage lasted for five torturous years, filled, she claimed, with her husband's recurrent nervous breakdowns and hospitalizations, culminating in him rejecting her love.

Anna was living in a small cottage she inherited in the picturesque town of Toms River, about thirty miles south of my sister's house in Holmdel. The area was wondrously watery, filled with the Toms River that wound through it, swamps, back bays, and finally the Jersey shoreline.

We dated, two emotional cripples awash in our own brand of anxiety. I would borrow, with her blessing, my sister's dead husband's VW Bug and, on Saturday mornings, drive to Toms River to meet Anna at her house. We then ventured up the Jersey Turnpike, through the Lincoln Tunnel, and into Manhattan, where we spent the afternoon at one museum or another. The Metropolitan Museum of Art and MOMA were our favorites. Once in a while, we spent the afternoon at a movie for a change of pace. In the evening, it was off to Little Italy for dinner before driving back to Toms River for sex and sleep. Sunday mornings, weather allowing, we drove to a local beach for a picnic brunch and a performance by the Atlantic Ocean, churning with winter's white-capped waves. We were enjoying life. By evening, I was back in Holmdel and back with my sister.

Anna made up most of my social life, but there was also my cousin on my mother's side, David. David lived with his first wife, Jennifer, off of the Frederick Law Olmsted-designed Ocean Parkway. David's work career was unsteady. What *was* steady were his wheelings and dealings, his fiddling with his beloved violin, and his avid attachment to bicycling. David was also a devotee of caregiving and I was in need of such care—at this juncture in my life we were made for each other.

Every Monday morning, my sister would drive me to Holmdel's New Jersey transit train station to catch the local to Penn Station in Manhattan. From there, I took the E train south to West 4th Street in the heart of Greenwich Village. David managed a futon store for a Russian Jewish immigrant at 8th Street and 2nd Avenue. It was a fifteen-minute walk to the store from the subway. The buzz of the city, watching the pedestrians and cars crowding the sidewalks and streets, was better than shock therapy to excite my brain and lift my spirits. Around the corner from David's futon store was, for some obscure reason, a street accessible electrical outlet. This led to a brisk trade in purloined electric appliances of all sorts as it allowed the sellers to demonstrate their wares to unscrupulous buyers. Two blocks further down 8th Street, at St. Marks Place, bicycle thieves and their cliental held their own illicit marketplace.

Under David's care, I would find a comfortable futon in the store's loft area to sleep or read on until closing time. No customer could leave the store without David introducing me, promoting opportunities for kibitzing, or gossiping.

David biked to work so when we headed to his apartment in Brooklyn, he took his bike down on the subway. Jen, his wife, had been a professional ballet dancer, though she was now out of work. She and I got along well—which was necessary, because on Monday nights I stayed over, eating dinner with them, sleeping on their living room couch. Jen was having her own emotional problems too. At times, she also showed up on Mondays at David's store, and then the two of us perched together in the store's loft, two birds in futon nests.

On Tuesdays, David had most of the day off. We would go biking in Brooklyn—my first time back on a bike in twenty-five years. Down the 100-year-old Ocean Parkway bike path we'd go, all the way to its conclusion at the latest Russian conquest in the new world: Brighten Beach. From there it was up on to the boardwalk and pedaling along the beach to Coney Island where we'd stop at Nathan's Famous for a hot dog smothered in relish and tubed in tart yellow mustard. On our way back to David's apartment, we stopped to visit my maternal grandparents at Washington Cemetery and then again at Marion's apartment. Marion was David's sister and also my first cousin. We'd end our trip with a visit to a *glatt* kosher restaurant for dessert.

I was slowly getting better. My sister, my cousin Marion, my younger brother who handled my finances, Anna, David, the little old lady psychiatrist, the Atlantic Ocean, Manhattan, Brooklyn, Ocean Parkway, Pamelor, David's loaner bicycle, Nathan's Hot Dogs, and my dead grandparents all conspired to move me forward. Finally, I was ready to go back on my own, back to Minnesota. It was difficult telling Anna I was leaving, and it smacked of betrayal even though I repeatedly told her I would eventually be leaving New Jersey. But we had been so good for each other. She didn't want it to end. Neither did I, but I knew Dan was right. Time-out was over.

Back in Minnesota, my goal was to restart my medical career. Fortunately, I had compulsively renewed my medical license. To solve the gloom and isolation I felt in my house, I advertised for UMN students to rent out my two available bedrooms. A congenial couple from Croatia responded. Just like that, my house came alive. As an added benefit, the female half of the couple, Mirianna, had soft, playful eyes, a young woman's lithe figure, and a sexy accent. I dreamed of her.

For all the good things that had happened, all the loving support I had received, I was still too close to my state of desperation to believe it was gone forever. Years before, when I had lived and worked in the rural town of Onamia, I became good friends with Larry Hill, the hospital's nurse anesthetist. Through him, I met his parents and became familiar with Larry's three siblings, all of whom suffered from genetically transmitted muscular dystrophy. The parents cared for all three siblings with TLC and didn't let go until death did them part. In the basement of their house was a bedroom, which, when I came back from New Jersey, they offered to me if I needed it. They wanted to care for me, to love and shelter me in my time of need. I took a good look at that basement bedroom, imprinted the sanctuary in my mind and used it as my ace in the hole. It was my backstop, my Plan B. I didn't end up using it, but knowing it was there was the kind of comfort I needed. It reminded me of patients I treated for panic attacks by prescribing Xanax. They often told me that once they knew the Xanax would faithfully quell their attack, they could abort a panic attack by just knowing that they had a Xanax tablet nearby, ready and available as needed.

While my license to practice medicine was valid, I wasn't ready to jump into seeing patients after an eighteen-year hiatus. I had spent ten of those years as a venture capitalist, about as far afield as I could get from being a doctor. A colleague of mine straight out warned me: "You can't make it back into practice. You missed out on almost two decades of rapid fire changes in medicine." I saw no other choice but to try.

I tried to find a residency program that would take me on for a year of training. I knew all the players at the academic hospitals in the Twin Cities, and I reached out to everyone I could. The response to my queries was always the same: "There's no way you'll fit in here. You're too out of the box." The last of a half dozen rejections came with a poignant bit of advice: "Just go back into practice and leave us alone!"

One of my good friends, a doctor and a true manic depressive, offered to let me shadow him as he saw patients at the clinic where he worked in Monticello, Minnesota. I rummaged through my storage boxes, found and dusted off my stethoscope—the design of which hadn't changed in fifty years—and prepared for what I hadn't done for eighteen years. Seeing patients. There I was, a 51-year-old medical student, hesitatingly examining those patients who agreed to provide me with an educational experience. Most did, it turned out. "Hold your breath so I can hear your heart," I'd say. "Take a deep breath so I can hear your lungs. Lie still so I can hear your intestines doing their thing." Slowly, I began to be comfortable with patients again, striking up conversations, feeling like my old doctor self.

After three weeks of following my buddy around, the clinic manager approached me. One of the clinic doctors was sick and missing in action. "Do you have an active license?" the manager asked me.

"Yes, I do."

"Well, why don't you fill in for Dr. X today? He has a full schedule I would hate to cancel. We'll pay you for each patient you see."

Whiz-bang—I was thrust back into being Dr. Zuckerman. I was afraid, determined not to make a mistake. That was paramount, more so than being of help to the patients. Diagnosing wasn't the problem—symptoms and signs hadn't changed much for most conditions. But the drug world was alien. The physicians' desk reference was my drug information Bible.

And then it happened. The clinic manager asked me into his office. "An elderly woman was in the clinic today and said she recognized you. She was supposed to see you as a patient and refused. She said you were a nut case she met when she was locked up in the psych ward at the University of Minnesota Hospital some four months ago. Is that true?"

I was shocked, frightened that my budding return to practice would be over just as it was getting started. I also felt betrayed. I remembered the old lady; we were soul-buddies at the University. How could she turn against me?

"I need to report you to my boss at Allina who owns the clinic," the manager explained. I anticipated the worst.

The head of Allina Clinic and I met at the Abbott Hospital in Minneapolis. "Is it true that you were hospitalized at the University of Minnesota Psych Ward four months ago?"

"Yes."

"How are you doing now?"

"Fine."

"I need proof that you're well enough to practice. A letter from a psychiatrist would do the trick. Are you seeing one?"

"I am," I told him. "It was part of my discharge plan that I see a psychiatrist monthly for at least six months. In fact, I had already asked him for just such a letter in case my suitability to practice was questioned. He had no problem writing that I was a-okay".

"Get me a copy of that letter and you can keep seeing patients at the clinic."

I felt a rush of relief, knowing that I would no longer have to worry about hiding my past.

I prepared to leave, but the clinic head then did me the biggest favor. "I should tell you that I have a similar diagnosis and am under treatment," he said. "I know where you're coming from."

Chapter 24: Epiphany

It's 2014 and I can't get "Take the 'A' Train," by Duke Ellington out of my head. Elgin, my nurse at Aspen East Lake Street Clinic, is from Harlem, though not from the Sugar Hill section. He hears me singing one day, and I promise to take him back to NYC so he and I can ride the A Train together. We'll travel from Greenwich Village, where I have a pied-à-terre studio apartment, all the way up to his old neighborhood.

"The subway fare is on me, Elgin. We'll catch the A at West 4th Street and take it all the way to 116th Street, humming 'Take the 'A' Train' all the way." He smiles; his memories of his youth in Harlem are sweet, filled with close neighbors and friends.

I bought my studio apartment in Greenwich Village back in the mid-90s, when New York real-estate prices had tanked and even Donald Trump was bankrupt and on an allowance provided by his "on the hook" bankers. The price was right: $54,000 for 500 square feet. The building at the corner of West 9th Street and 6th Avenue came with a doorman and an elevator and was four entertaining Greenwich Village blocks from the Northwest entrance to Washington Square Park.

My studio's two windows faced west and out onto 6th Avenue, providing a view of the Jefferson Market Library and its community garden. Once a courthouse, with an attached women's detention center famous for trying Mae West on obscenity charges, the building has been a library since 1967. It's now a national landmark, never to be torn down, its bell tower ringing out across the Lower West Side since it was put back in action in 1996.

I dreamed of living in that apartment, writing and roaming the West Village streets. Trouble was my son moved into the studio within months of my purchase, followed shortly thereafter by his girlfriend/wife-to-be. They were quickly married, and then came their two children. When their eldest daughter outgrew her dresser-drawer bed, their family was off to affordable Brooklyn—or at least affordable back then. But before I could reclaim my apartment, my daughter moved in. I am still on the waiting list.

Elgin and I met at East Lake Street Clinic, the people's clinic, one of many voices, that served the aging Longfellow neighborhood of South Minneapolis. Traditionally, the neighborhood was home to blue-collar workers of Scandinavian heritage. By the time I started working at East Lake, the neighborhood had been transformed into a melting pot in the midst of the white gentrification that was happening in most of the city. Native Americans, African Americans, Somalis, Ethiopians, Mexican immigrants, starving artists, and the aging remnants of the original blue-collar families now shared community in Longfellow.

East Lake Street took in lost souls, and Elgin and I were no exception. Neither of us had practiced within our respective fields for at least a decade, but the clinic gave us both another chance—as it did for so many of those in need within its reach.

Despite how welcome I felt at East Lake Street, my recent lack of experience did come up as a potential issue. Shortly after I was hired, I came across a memo addressed to my fellow doctor Merrill Davis that was clearly not meant for my eyes. "Keep an eye on Zuckerman," it read. "Let me know if there is any problem." It was signed by Aspen's Medical Director. As much as I felt slighted by the memo, the author was right; I needed oversight, and not only by my own conscience.

So many new drugs had come on the market since I last wrote a prescription (Rx) that I ended up feeling lost in a sea of potent chemicals. "Please excuse me, I'll be back in a minute," I told each patient. I would then run to my office to frantically search my pharmacopeia. "Yes, yes, that's the right dosage of Digoxin. Is it safe to give with the myriad of drugs the patient is already on? Check the potassium level first. If it's low, Digoxin could kill the patient! I haven't checked kidney tests. *Warning: decrease the dose of Digoxin if the patient has kidney problems.* Oh boy, this is scary stuff."

Then, one day, two years after restarting practice, I realized I was comfortable prescribing. I no longer needed to reference my pharmacopeia for every patient. It was a eureka moment that left me feeling like Sir Isaac Newton, who came to realize that an apple falling was not just an average occurrence but was, instead, a phenomenon.

East Lake Street's roster of employee's reflected the colors of its neighborhood. Some of the staff actually lived close by. My fellow physicians and I mostly lived in other neighborhoods, but we all shared a passion for being needed, to use our skills to help those less privileged. The suburbs, the middle class and above didn't really need us. East Lake Street clients did. On the rare occasions when a well-to-do suburbanite would stray into my office, I had to switch gears, switch lingo, and switch effort. Once adjusted, their care was a snap.

"I see you are on so and so medication, do you know what for?" I'd ask as an opener.

"X is for my hypertension, Y is for my gastritis, Z is for my elevated cholesterol. I take them before breakfast. I have a pill dispenser. I hope to get off X and Z by exercise and weight loss. Yes, I belong to a club. So far I'm down fifteen pounds; I'm trying to avoid becoming diabetic like my mother. No, I never smoked. Oh yeah, I tried marijuana twice in college. Drink? Coca Cola! By the way, I want to update my pneumonia vaccine and I believe I am old enough to get my insurance company to pay for a shingles' vaccine. My wife keeps badgering me to get another colonoscopy. My last one was five years ago and I told her it isn't time yet—I've still got five years to go! Hey, by the way, your waiting area is a mess. It could use some sprucing up."

The Voice helped me understand that it was my inclination, my calling, to be of help to others. A big part of that calling was to help those in need change for the better through one-on-one, intimate encounters. What better vehicle to fulfill my life's work than to practice primary care, where almost all the action occurred one-on-one?

I called my office the "medical confessional booth," as it almost felt religious when I met with a patient. Like a priest who was well suited for his job, I was full of curiosity and a desire to know my patients, to know what their symptoms felt like, their tics, their foibles, their genius. I wanted to mingle my soul with theirs, for us to truly love one another.

As a teenager I was exposed to the Actors' Studio in Manhattan where Marlon Brando and others studied Lee Strasberg's method acting. The glamour of being an actor called to me. Stage fright, the fear of forgetting my lines, scared me away. Nonetheless, I was inspired by theatrics. The two drama heroes of my youth were my mother and the ever antic Dr. Gabriel Kirschenbaum, my childhood family practitioner and Williamsburg don.

Early on in my medical career I had taken a seminar entitled "Acting for Non-Actors" taught by a professional actor I was friends with. The seminar was marketed mainly to uptight salesmen to help them communicate more effectively, instill confidence, close deals. I had already turned my office into a medical confessional booth, but the seminar opened my eyes to the fact that I also unwittingly turned it into a theatrical arena.

It was natural for me to relate to almost any of my patients on a personal level, to change roles like a chameleon, change lingo, to match my patients' personalities and needs. I had done it all, or at least it seemed that way. I was brought up in Jewish Brooklyn in the 1940s, lived in Greenwich Village, in Haight-Ashbury at the height of the Haight. I spent two years in Truk Island, Micronesia, practicing medicine amongst tribal people and swimming with real sharks. I had lived in rural Minnesota amongst Native Americans, worked as a lifeguard, a counselor, a racetrack cashier, and a bricklayer's assistant on a job in Brooklyn where the bricklayer's union was mafia controlled. I practiced as a small town physician, ran a non-profit rural hospital and physician co-op that I founded. I also started and ran three venture capital funds and sat on multiple boards of for-profit and non-profit organizations. As a teenager I had been a Manhattan subway champ, capable of beating old ladies to empty rush hour seats. I was a letterman in swimming in high school and college—though, admittedly, not a very fast one. I'd been deemed crazy and locked up in a mental institution for three months. At age forty I was told I had a fatal form of intestinal cancer and for weeks I went through all the emotional trauma of expecting to die, and eventually accepting my own death, only to learn that it was a false diagnosis. I've been married and divorced and remarried. I have two grown children, two grandchildren, and I've written two books full of philosophical humor. These experiences cultivated my soul, allowed me to be open to patients who were from all walks of life, all religions and races, with different values and desires—ones facing imminent death, emotional meltdown, or were simply fellow humans. Once they entered my office, I adapted to them, becoming whatever doctor they needed me to be. I may not have made it to the stage, but I created my own within those office walls.

*

One day at East Lake Street, I go to open the door of my examining room to see my next patient: a 23-year-old redneck construction worker. I've seen him before for minor ailments. He and I talked about his work and my experience as a bricklayer's assistant in the old days in Brooklyn. When I open the door, there he is, sitting in my chair with his feet up on my desk. Sitting in the patient's chair is someone who could have been his twin. I stare at the patient with disdain, but he doesn't budge. "Hey Doc, how you doing?" he boisterously chimes out. Now I'm fuming, but instead of ranting at him I decide it's best to retreat. I get to the threshold of the room, then I stop. I know this lout, I know what he wants, what he expects from me.

I turn around, re-enter my office and confront my patient. "If you don't get your smelly feet off my desk in three seconds I'm going to throw you and your buddy out the window!" Never mind that there is no window in my office.

The patient immediately removes his feet and turns to his buddy. "That's my doc!" he proudly proclaims.

On another day, the patient is a 16-year-old boy who is clearly physically underdeveloped and, I suspect, mentally disabled as well. He is accompanied by his father who does all the talking. I tread lightly; the father is obviously anguished by his son's condition. Lots of tests have been done on the patient with no conclusive evidence as to what's wrong with him.

This is the first time I have seen either the patient or the father. Regardless, I have an inkling of how to help—or at least how to draw out the truth. "I wish we doctors were smarter than we are," I say. "So we could tell you exactly what's wrong with your son and how to help him." I follow my statement with a sizeable pregnant pause.

After four or five seconds the father says: "I have to tell you the truth. I've been so embarrassed, so ashamed of myself, that I never told anyone that my son suffers from congenital syphilis. That's what he has, that's what he suffers from."

Another day, a Jewish nursing home patient is in for a visit. She's an elderly lady with all her marbles. I note in the chart that she visits the clinic monthly, seeing a different doctor almost every time. I have never seen her before. She's had multiple complaints, but a battery of tests have all come back normal enough. I greet the patient and go to sit down. As I do, I loudly exclaim, "Oy vey!"

"What's wrong doctor?" the patient asks with sincere concern.

I then launch into a litany of bogus medical conditions I claim to be suffering from. The patient listens intently to my every word. Finally I say, "But you're not hear to listen to my problems. What's bothering you today?"

"Never you mind, Doctor," she says. "You have too many problems. I'll come back some other time."

I assume the theatrics worked by giving the patient exactly what she really wanted: a thrill to punctuate her boring existence.

Tap into the soul, melt away the defenses, love the patient as yourself, and out pours the real problem, the hidden diagnosis. After uncovering the truth, the patient opens up and suddenly they're willing to undergo tests, take befuddling medications, see specialists, even lose weight, exercise, and stop smoking.

How I loved my practice, my patients, and was loved back by them. I began to feel connected to them on another level, which led to some almost-supernatural encounters.

It started as a sudden sensation of joy, of exaltation that took my breath away and made me want to cry. I was sitting in front of a patient one day and all of a sudden I felt speechless, overwhelmed by what was happening inside me. I tried to hide the tears streaming down my face, down onto my nostrils, but my patient noticed. I couldn't explain what had just happened. The patient had been speaking about his family, whom he deeply cherished, and suddenly it was like I could feel the same love that he must be feeling welling up inside of me. Was I too emotionally involved in his stories and therefore generating the feelings, the tears through my own empathy?

It began to happen over and over. Most of the time I'd just be interviewing my patients, not feeling much of anything, until wham! A wall of loving emotions would hit me, enough to leave me in tears. I just knew this overwhelming sensation wasn't coming from me. It had to be the patient who somehow made me aware of how they were feeling. After having been mentored by The Voice in my deaf ear, I was no longer immune to the magical workings of the universe around me. I realized that when the patients spoke of people they cared dearly about, their feelings must be transmitted non-verbally. My brain must be picking up on these feelings, causing me to have an involuntary physical reaction.

I decided to call it an epiphany experience. Epiphanies were moments of insight, of realization, and that was exactly how I felt: flooded with joy, as though I was discovering the secrets of the universe.

Then, one day, a different sensation ambushed me. It was a buzzing, irritating sensation, varying in strength. Like the epiphany experience, it occurred during a conversation with a patient. It was contact, but not the loving kind. This one filled me with an angst-like sensation. I must have struck a chord, an unhappy and problematic one, and the patient was letting me know. It started to come just as frequently as the epiphany experience, the joy and the unhappiness coursing through my emotional being when I least expected it.

But epiphany and angst sensations were not all that was happening. To my surprise, one day I discovered that I was reading the minds of my patients—and other people's too! It all started when I began to recognize weird thoughts that popped into my head while talking with people. At first, I buried these aberrancies, assuming they were self-generated, but it didn't make any sense. The thoughts were so foreign to me—there was no way it was my own stray musings.

Me: "Where is your husband today? Usually he's always with you."

Patient: "He decided to go shopping while I was waiting to see you."

Me: *Grapefruits suddenly come to mind. Go ahead, take a swing at it, don't be ashamed, feed the patient that thought and see what happens.* "Is he going to buy grapefruits?"

Patient: "Oh, thank you for reminding me, that's what I forgot to tell him to

buy."

Another encounter:

Patient: "The tests will have to wait, we're off on vacation tomorrow."

Me: *Aruba's on my mind.* "I bet you're going to Aruba."

Patient: "How did you know?"

Another time, a patient was in for a pre-op for her cataract surgery. I started to say: "You're only fifty. Did your ophthalmologist explain to you why you have cataracts at age fifty?"

But that's not what I said. I got a brain twitch and decided to go with it. "You're only fifty. Did your ophthalmologist explain why you have Cadillacs at age fifty?"

The patient hesitated, then smiled at me. "At age eight or nine, I had a cat I loved dearly and it needed surgery. I ran to tell my grandfather about the operation. Princess is going to have Cadillac surgery tomorrow, I told him. Grandfather laughed heartedly."

As more and more of these strange, inexplicable experiences occurred, I became convinced that there was no way I could know things about my patients without them somehow transmitting this information to me non-verbally. Was I telepathic? Was I picking up brain beams? How would that even work?

Just like with The Voice, there was no clear-cut scientific explanation. There will always be those miraculous things in the world that no one can explain. I thought and thought about my "mind reading," about the epiphany and angst experiences. What instinctually came to me was that thoughts and feelings could be transmitted from a patient's brain down their optic nerves to their eyes where they would be beamed out to me. My eyes would receive these transmissions and, along with light waves, send the information through my optic nerve to my brain.

    It might sound crazy and of course to date is scientifically unproven, but it is well accepted that the eyes transfer lots of feelings non-verbally, that they are supposed to be the windows to the soul. In Matthew 6:22-23, Jesus says, "The light of the body is in the eye. If therefore thine eye be single, thy whole body shall be full of light…But if thine eye be evil, thy whole body shall be full of darkness." Is all eye language due to ocular muscles changing an eye's appearance, pupillary dilatation and contraction, iris patterns, changing dimensions of the whites of the eye, or the eyes somehow causing a release of oxytocin, the love hormone? Or could it be something more far out, like the brain beams that have yet to be discovered. Of course, I must be a transmitter of "brain-eye communication" as well as a receiver. Is the chemical communication of the amoeba partially replaced by brain-eye communication? What I couldn't deny was real—whatever the cause—were the strange things that kept happening to me.

*

"Lyphing Dancer comes out of the gate smartly from the number three hole and takes the early lead!" The track announcer blared out rapid fire. "Coming into the stretch, Lyphing Dancer is still two lengths in the lead!"

I was shaking with emotion.

"Hold on, hold on you sob!" I shouted.

"Lyphing Dancer goes wire to wire to win the 1 1/16 mile third race!" the announcer screamed.

It was that morning, back on February 16th, 1991, that the name "Lyphing Dancer" was touted to me by The Voice.

Actually, the tout came in a time period just prior to The Voice's appearance, a period of wonder and strangeness, when all my senses seemed heightened. The world was illuminated by a different, more brilliant light. Then one morning, this premonition just appeared in my mind: *A horse with a name similar to Lightning Dancer will win a Pick Six race today at Golden Gate Field.*

Excited, I searched the race listings in the newspaper, scouring all of the Pick Six races. Nothing resembled "Lighting Dancer." The premonition was so clear, so precise, how could it not be true? Could the horse be a late entry? Was there a misprint in the paper? Think, think, think. And then it struck me. It was Sunday, and the Pick Six starts in the third race, not the fourth. Trembling, I scanned the entries for Race 3. There it was! Lyphing Dancer, a name almost identical to the one that had appeared in my head.

At the time of the premonition, I was still in my pajamas, busy cleaning the kitchen after breakfast. I had no intention of going to the track. Now I had no choice: I had to bet on Lyphing Dancer to win. How could I not?

"I'll put $200 on his nose," I told myself as I drove to Canterbury Downs in a daze. "He's four to one in the morning line, which means I could win $800." I arrived in plenty of time to bet the simulcast of the third race from Golden Gates Field. The odds on Lyphing Dancer had risen to seven to one. Clearly, no one else had gotten the same premonition.

I was shaking with excitement, anticipation. "How are you doing?" I asked a seemingly downtrodden black man who was studiously reviewing his racing form.

"Lousy," he responded.

At first, I hesitated. Then I said, "Try the number three horse in the third race at Golden Gate. Bet him to win, Lyphing Dancer. You can't go wrong."

"Thanks. He can't do any worse than the nags I've been picking," the man said.

The betting line was twenty deep, but time was on my side. Suddenly, I was in the front of the betting window. *This is crazy, it isn't really happening,* I told myself. *I don't want to lose $200. This premonition could be a test, a set-up to teach me not to try to make money betting on a horse.*

"Fifty dollars on Lyphing Dancer," I finally blurted out to the teller. "I mean number three. Yes, at Golden Gate Fields. Yes, to win."

Of course Lyphing Dancer won. The whole time I sat on the edge of my seat, my heart in my throat. By the time the race was over, I was left with heartburn and a profit of $375. If I had only bet $200, I would have won $1,500. I was a seventy-five percent disbeliever.

Predicting the winner of a horse race isn't the same as Nostradamus predicting the vague rise of the antichrist sometime in the distant future. It is a precision predication, the outcome measured in parts of inches, in the here and now and with monetary consequences. Lyphing Dancer's victory still inspires and astounds me, and makes me believe that the spiritual world exists. Because of my time with The Voice and everything else that has happened to me over the past twenty-five years I now believe that we humans can transcend our individual mortal beings and be at one with the spiritual universe, with The Blur, with G-d, where all is love.

Epilogue

Of course, I never got another winner, another Lyphing Dancer. The lesson was learned; another winner would only serve to make money. If I didn't chicken out on my way to bet, that is. But money was never the point—trusting in the spiritual, in *myself*, was.

I have been fortunate to have lived a life of fulfillment. By hook or by crook, I became what I was destined to be. A doctor first, but also a businessman and a writer. I never thought I would be famous or fabulously wealthy, except in my fantasy world. I was gifted in math, but what interested me was people, not calculus. Medicine, caring for people one-on-one, was my fulfillment. Being Dr. Zuckerman was my ticket.

Does The Voice ever talk to me in my left ear anymore? No. We merged; The Voice is me now. But that doesn't stop me from teasing Pamela, my wife of fourteen years, telling her The Voice has spoken to me and told me to do this, or not do that. "Don't tell me The Voice told you that you don't have to take out the garbage!" she shrieks. I love her for her defiance, for her not allowing me to become a prophet in my own marriage!

None of it was easy: my time with Madelaine, The Voice in my head that drove me to revelation, the time spent locked up in mental institutions. But looking back, I wouldn't change any of it. I have come to the belief that I am the author of my trials and tribulation. I flirted with ruination, with hopelessness, in order to know the joy of survival and of overcoming, of rebirth. Am I a head amoeba? It really doesn't matter anymore. What matters is being *me*, being able to share my experience with The Voice, to exude my brand of love and humor in the hope of stimulating other open-minded humans to achieve that ultimate conjugal experience, the oneness with G-d: epiphany.

The Horse Race

GOLDEN GATE FIELDS - February 16, 1991 - Race 3
CLAIMING - Thoroughbred
Claiming Price: $6,250 - $0
One And One Sixteenth Miles On The Dirt
Purse: $7,000
Available Money: $7,000
Value of Race: $7,000 1st $3,850, 2nd $1,400, 3rd $1,050, 4th $525, 5th $175
Weather: Clear Track: Fast
Off at: : Start: Good for all except

Last Raced	Pgm	Horse Name (Jockey)	Wgt M/E	PP	Start	1/4	1/2	3/4	Str	Fin	Odds	Comments
10Feb91 4GG1	3	Lyphing Dancer (Valenzuela, Fernando)	117 BL b	3	1	$1^{1/2}$	$1^{1/2}$	$1^{1 1/2}$	1^4	1^7	7.50	ridd'n out; good spd
26Jan91 4GG5	8	Monsier Frijoles (Sibille, Ray)	117 BL b	8	8	8^1	$7^{1 1/2}$	7^{Head}	$2^{1 1/2}$	2^2	17.70	2nd best; wide trip
21Jan91 5BM8	5	Texas Day (Doocy, Timothy)	117 L b	5	2	$4^{1 1/2}$	3^{Head}	$3^{1/2}$	3^{Head}	3^1	35.60	stalked pace no rally
9Feb91 5GG4	4	Rodney's Gold (Hansen, Ron)	117 BL bf	4	6	$7^{1 1/2}$	$5^{1/2}$	$4^{1/2}$	$4^{1 1/2}$	4^2	1.40*	svd grnd
24Jan91 5GG2	2	Rare Sassafras (Gonzalez, Roberto)	117 BL	2	4	3^{Head}	4^{Head}	$6^{1 1/2}$	5^1	5^5	5.00	no factor; rail trip
25Jan91 5BM6	1	Renegado (Lamance, Chris)	117 L b	1	5	8	8	8	7^1	6^7	39.40	outrun; slw early
11Jan91 5BM5	7	Splendid Hypa (Snyder, Bartley)	112? L b	7	3	2^2	2^{Head}	$2^{1 1/2}$	8^{Head}	7^1	3.20	faltered; roughed
26Jan91 4GG2	6	Mirrors (Patterson, Alan)	117 BL bl	6	7	5^{Head}	6^{Head}	$5^{1/2}$	8	8	5.80	stopped; btwn rvls

Fractional Times: 22.50 46.50 1:10.90 1:35.90 Final Time: 1:42.30
Split Times: (24:00) (24:40) (25:00) (6:40)
Run-Up: 0 feet

Winner: Lyphing Dancer, Chestnut Gelding, by Clignancourt (FR) out of Break Even, by Gunter. Foaled May 23, 1987 in California.
Breeder: Spiro Pettas. **Winning Owner:** O'Neill W J

Claiming Prices: 3 - Lyphing Dancer: $6,250; 8 - Monsier Frijoles: $6,250; 5 - Texas Day: $6,250; 4 - Rodney's Gold: $6,250; 2 - Rare Sassafras: $6,250; 1 - Renegado: $6,250; 7 - Splendid Hypa: $6,250; 6 - Mirrors: $6,250;

Total WPS Pool: $0

Pgm	Horse	Win	Place	Wager Type	Winning Numbers	Payoff	Pool
3	Lyphing Dancer						
8	Monsier Frijoles						
5	Texas Day						

Past Performance Running Line Preview

Pgm	Horse Name	Start	1/4	1/2	3/4	Str	Fin
3	Lyphing Dancer	1	$1^{1/2}$	$1^{1/2}$	$1^{1 1/2}$	1^4	1^7
8	Monsier Frijoles	8	$6^{4 1/4}$	$7^{1 1/2}$	7^5	2^5	2^7
5	Texas Day	2	$4^{2 1/2}$	$3^{1/2}$	3^3	$5^{3 1/2}$	3^6
4	Rodney's Gold	6	$7^{5 1/4}$	$5^{3/4}$	$4^{3 1/2}$	$4^{5 1/2}$	4^{10}
2	Rare Sassafras	4	$3^{2 1/2}$	$4^{3/4}$	$6^{4 1/2}$	5^7	5^{12}
1	Renegado	5	$8^{3 3/4}$	8^3	8^6	$7^{10 1/4}$	6^{20}
7	Splendid Hypa	3	$2^{1/2}$	$2^{1/2}$	$2^{1 1/2}$	6^{12}	7^{92}
6	Mirrors	7	5^4	$6^{1 1/4}$	5^5	$8^{11 1/4}$	8^{23}

Trainers: 3 - Greenman, Walter; 8 - Trinchard, Barry; 5 - Utley, Doug; 4 - Webb, Bryan; 2 - Mastrangelo, William; 1 - Utley, Doug; 7 - Amescua, Rene; 6 - Wingfield, Robert

Owners: 3 - O'Neill W J; 8 - Murphy Mrs W J; 5 - Robinson & Troxell; 4 - Mt High Stable & Carrigan; 2 - Mastrangelo & White; 1 - L C Mcelhinney; 7 - Syndicate Stable; 6 - Andrea L Sanders;

Footnotes

Acknowledgements

As I started to write these acknowledgements, I became filled with joy at realizing all those who have inspired and helped me give birth to this book. It is with warm pleasure that I acknowledge those souls who carried my spirit forward.

In my case, there were more than the usual forces at play. For me, The

Voice—mine and G-d's—was pivotal to this story and must be acknowledged.

Though Madelaine is not her real name, my girlfriend at the time was my protagonist who not only provoked my emotional instability, but from whom I learned and inherited traits and truths that transformed me. I can only wish her well at a distance.

My first editor, Stephanie Ericcson, vicariously lived my tale for ten years. She, as much as The Voice, dug into me and brought forth the truth. My present editor, Rachel Carter, helped bring my fifteen year authorship odyssey to culmination and to my publisher's doorstep.

My patients—my fellow mountebanks—kept expanding, to my joy, the scope of my appreciation, my love, for humanity.

My present wife of fourteen years, Pamela, and I see many things differently. We argue, we make up, we argue again, and I am driven to invent new visions. Such was also the case with my first wife, Kathleen. I might not have learned much from women in my first twenty-five years of life, but I've certainly made up for that over the past fifty years.

This book already addresses the roles my mother, father and siblings played in helping to ground me. As well as how my dear friend Marshall helped to make me a medical missionary. No more is needed to be said about them.

As for my children, Gabrielle and Joshua, they were my prime reason not to accept death or commit suicide. They needed me, their father. Not so much anymore, but I'm still grateful for every moment we've spent together.

Biography

Stephen L. Zuckerman was born in Williamsburg, Brooklyn, New York City. At the tender age of three, he was influenced to go into medicine by an extraordinary and at times outrageous mentor, Dr. Gabriel Kirshenbaum, a bear of a man who took care of his neighbors and patients like they were his own cubs. He attended Stuyvesant High School, the boiler of brilliance in Manhattan, and like all the students there, believed he was meant for great things.

He attended medical school at the State University of New York in Brooklyn, a Woody Allen school full of first and second-generation Jewish and Italian neurotics, driven by their families to become doctors.

His medical residency was at Mt. Zion Hospital in the Fillmore district of San Francisco, the hippie center for rebellious doctors in the late sixties. At Mt Zion he became the first person to be reported suffering from secondary marijuana smoke intoxication.

After his rowdy residency years Dr. Zuckerman and his wife and two children spent two years on Truk

Island, where he worked as a staff physician and head of diving medicine for the United Nations Trust Territories of the Pacific. During this time, he underwent a major paradigm shift, brought on by his contact with the so-called primitive peoples of Truk and the other Micronesian Islanders he encountered.

In 1981, Dr. Zuckerman lurched from being a medical missionary to a venture capital mercenary. He wasn't greedy enough to be a great success, but nevertheless earned his keep, and for ten years found adventure. When the adventure ran out, desperate, he returned to his first love of medicine, ready to fill Dr. Kirschenbaum's shoes. For the next twenty-three years, Dr. Z., as he was lovingly called, was Dr. Kirschenbaum on speed. None of his patients escaped his infectious humor or enveloping zest for life.

If you enjoyed this book, would you be kind enough to leave a review on Amazon? Click Here

Check out some of my other work, including – *Medical Humor at Its Best!* and *Doc, What's Up?* Now available in paperback or eBook.

Like me on Facebook:

www.facebook.com/drstephenzuckerman/

Check out my website at: www.zuckerisms.com

Find me on Twitter @Zuckerisms48

Thank You for Reading!

Made in the USA
Lexington, KY
26 February 2017